CONVERSION TO JUDAISM
IN JEWISH LAW

Essays and Responsa

STUDIES IN PROGRESSIVE HALAKHAH, VOLUME III

Also in this Series

Walter Jacob and Moshe Zemer (eds.) DYNAMIC JEWISH LAW,
Progressive Halakhah - Essence and Application

Walter Jacob and Moshe Zemer (eds.) RABBINIC - LAY
RELATIONS IN JEWISH LAW

CONVERSION TO JUDAISM
IN JEWISH LAW

Essays and Responsa

Edited by
Walter Jacob and Moshe Zemer

Freehof Institute of Progressive Halakhah
Tel Aviv and Pittsburgh
Rodef Shalom Press
1994

Published by the Rodef Shalom Press
4905 Fifth Avenue
Pittsburgh, PA 15213
U.S.A.

Copyright © 1994, Solomon B. Freehof Institute of Progressive Halakhah

4 Rehov Levitan
69204 Tel Aviv
Israel

4905 5th Avenue
Pittsburgh, PA 15213
U.S.A.

Library of Congress Catalog Card Number 93-074045

Jacob, Walter 1930-

Zemer, Moshe 1932-

ISBN 0-929699-05-X

This volume is dedicated

to

Ernest ז״ל and Ena Tarrasch
Arthur and Lena Rosen

and

Rabbi Robert and Annette Samuels
Rabbi Henry and Sheba Skirball
Rabbi Uri and Garri Regev

CONTENTS

PREFACE v

INTRODUCTION vii

HALAKHAH AND ULTERIOR MOTIVES - Rabbinic Discretion and the Law of Conversion
    Mark Washovsky 1

RETROACTIVE ANNULMENT OF A CONVERSION - A Survey of Representative Halakhic Sources
    David Ellenson 49

SINCERE CONVERSION AND ULTERIOR MOTIVES
    Bernard M. Zlotowitz 67

AMBIVALENCE IN PROSELYTISM
    Moshe Zemer 83

WITHOUT MILAH AND TEVILAH
    Richard Rosenthal 103

CONVERSION AND THE DEVELOPING REFORM HALAKHAH
    Walter Jacob 115

SELECTED REFORM RESPONSA

Conversion Without Formal Instruction 135
Gerut and the Question of Belief 141
Convert from Another Land 145
Conversion and Church Membership 147
Mental Competency of a Convert 151
The Pregnant Proselyte 153
Converting a Married Woman 157

Conversion of a Young Child 159
Circumcision of Proselytes 163
Prospective Convert who Fears Circumcision
and *Miqveh* 171
Convert and Hebrew 175
Miqveh and Reform Converts 177
Swimming Pool as a *Miqveh* 181
The Incomplete Conversion 185
Layman Conducting a Conversion 189
Privacy of a Convert 195
Unprovable Claims to Conversion 197
The Course of Study for *Gerut* 203
The Proselyte and Her Gentile Parents 205
Memorializing Christian Relatives 209
An Apostate Proselyte 213

CONTRIBUTORS 215

PREFACE

We wish to express special gratitude to our colleagues, Daniel Schiff, Debra Pine, and Joseph M. Glaser for their assistance with the proof reading of this volume. We also wish to thank Barbara Bailey for her help and Robert Goldman for his efforts in typesetting the manuscript. He has done a lot for the Institute over the years and we are grateful.

This volume and its predecessors would not have been possible without the generous gifts of Admiral Joshua Goldberg. We wish to express our special gratitude and wish him well.

INTRODUCTION

These essays explore conversion to Judaism and the issues connected with it in the late twentieth century. Our problems are very different from those of the past; they will be discussed in these pages.

Conversion to Judaism by individuals and groups has been part of the Jewish heritage from the early Biblical period onward, but not in our modern sense. In the Biblical period it meant joining a community more than a religion. We should note that even this was peripheral to other concerns.

In the patriarchal tales of the Bible, the stories of the conquest of Canaan, and the period of the judges and kings, however, conversion to Judaism remained a minor matter. Much more important was the dangerous attraction of other religions; the prophets consistently spoke about the problems which those religions caused the Israelites and Judeans.

The only militant effort at conversion to Judaism occurred during the period of the Maccabees (165-125 B.C.E.), when the Idumeans were forced to become Jews. Subsequently in the Roman Empire we sought converts through persuasion. Some historians feel that the Jewish communities of the Roman Empire consisted of more converts than of born Jews. In addition, many people were attracted to Judaism but never officially joined the Jewish People; those individuals called *Yirei Adonai* or *Gerei Tzedeq* were loosely identified with Judaism and sympathetic to its ideas. The number of such individuals in the Roman Empire as well as the size of the Jewish population in the Roman Empire remains an area of scholarly disagreement.

The Talmud reacted to those who converted to Judaism and those who sought to identify themselves with some portion of Jewish ethics and monotheism. The recorded reactions both positive and negative reflect historic circumstances, local events and personal experiences.

From the Council of Nicea (fourth century) and the later Fall of the Roman Empire until the middle of the nineteenth century, conversion to Judaism was rare and the subject was hardly discussed in Jewish circles. Attempts to convert us were, of course, made by the dominant Zoroastrian, Christian and Muslim communities which sought to force the Jewish minority into its fold. Jews, on the other hand, only rarely sought or succeeded in gaining converts. The most notable exception were the Khazars, a Southern Russian people whose ruling class converted to Judaism in the seventh or eighth century. This incident which seized the imagination of the oppressed and downtrodden Jewish community of Europe and North Africa was an isolated occurrence.

We did nothing to encourage conversion to Judaism during the Middle Ages as even a single convert could enrage the Christian world and bring about the destruction of a community. Some Christian and Muslim individuals nevertheless joined us; their members were very small and many of their names have, for that reason, been recorded.

The medieval codes of Jewish law dealt with converts and conversion but only briefly. There was no thorough discussion of these matters until the late nineteenth century when the Emancipation brought us into direct contact with the surrounding cultures of Europe and its inhabitants and conversion to Judaism began to occur.

In twentieth century America, and in other western lands, conversion to Judaism is no longer rare. We do not seek it through missionary efforts but welcome those who wish to join us. The larger number of converts has raised many issues about motivation, status, relationships with various segments of the Jewish community, requirements for conversion, etc. These essays, presented in San Antonio in nineteen ninety-two in a different form, should bring a better understanding of conversion to Judaism and its *halakhic* implications to the reader.

HALAKHAH AND ULTERIOR MOTIVES
Rabbinic Discretion and the Law of Conversion*

Mark Washofsky

Conversion to Judaism, according to *halakhah*, is an act which must be undertaken out of sincere religious motivations. The *baraita* (*Yeb.* 47a-b) which defines the conversion process requires that the prospective proselyte declare his readiness to join his fate to that of the Jewish people, even though this entails suffering and persecution. He or she is to be informed of some of the commandments and accept upon himself the obligation to keep them.[1] Another *tanaitic* source emphasizes that this acceptance be total; a non-Jew who is ready to follow all the commandments except for one is not to be converted.[2] Conversion contemplated for ulterior motives, be they fear and intimidation, hope of monetary gain, or desire to marry a Jew, does not fall within the category of religious sincerity. The validity of such conversions was long a matter of dispute, and a number of sources, *tanaitic* and later, regard these proselytes as Gentiles.[3] Even though the "final" *halakhah* recognizes their Jewishness,[4] this is justified as an after-the-fact (*bedi'avad*) necessity: perhaps, despite appearances to the contrary, these persons did convert for the proper religious reasons.[5] In principle (*lehatkhilah*), though, these conversions are not to be allowed, just as proselytes were not accepted in the days of David and Solomon and will not be accepted in the days of the Messiah, periods of history when Jewish power and prosperity, rather than devotion to Torah, are the putative reasons for a Gentile's wish to become a Jew.[6] The codifiers explicitly assume this line. Although a person who undergoes the conversion ritual is, after the fact, a valid *ger*, he should first be examined to see whether his decision is motivated by improper desires. Only if no such ulterior motive (money, fear, marriage) is discovered may we assume that he wishes to convert "for the sake of Heaven" (*leshem shamayim*) and accept him.[7]

The *halakhic* "codes", it is true, do not possess intrinsic authority. Unlike the codes of other legal systems, which are promulgated by recognized legislative bodies and are regarded as binding statements of the law, those in Jewish law more closely resemble legal textbooks that in the opinion of their authors render accurate descriptions of the law as it is derived from its real source, in our case the *Babylonian Talmud*.[8] Still, a clear and unequivocal description of the *halakhah* by the codifiers is a persuasive argument that the law is in fact according to their interpretation of it. It is significant, then, that the position sketched above is uncontested by the major codifiers. Nowhere do we find a declaration to the contrary, namely that the rabbinic court (*Bet Din*) may in principle accept for conversion those who come to us for the "wrong" reasons. To be sure, a certain amount of flexibility is built into the law. The *Tosafists*, for example, note that the *Talmud* records instances wherein Hillel and Rabbi Hiyya accepted converts who were driven by a desire for prestige or marriage. To resolve the apparent contradiction between the law and these two case rulings, the *Tosafists* suggest that the rabbis in question were certain that these proselytes would eventually adopt Judaism out of sincere religious motivations.[9] Later *posqim* (decisors) adopted this explanation, declaring that "we learn from here that the entire matter is left to the judgement of the court" (*hakol lefi re'ut einai Bet Din*).[10] Since this gloss has made its way into the annotated editions of the "codes", we must adjust our statement of the mainstream *halakhic* position as follows: those wishing to become Jews out of ulterior motives are ineligible for conversion, but the decision in each individual case is left to the discretion of the rabbinical authorities on the scene.

The word "discretion" raises an important theoretical issue concerning the nature of judicial decision-making. A large body of literature in the field of jurisprudence is devoted to the question of judicial discretion: to what extent is the judge empowered to choose an answer-in effect, to make new law-in a case which comes before him for decision?[11] It is generally held that, in legal systems where the law is authoritatively formulated in literary sources, the judge's task is to apply to the case at hand the applicable written rule of law. That rule may be stated explicitly in the texts, or it may exist implicitly, "between the lines" of the written sources, to be derived through the use of logic, analogy, or other tools of legal reasoning accepted as valid by the system's practitioners.[12] Frequently, a judge will confront a question for which the texts provide no one obviously correct answer. How he renders a decision in the case is the subject of dispute between the various jurisprudential schools of thought. Legal positivists, for whom law is a system of rules enacted by authorized legislators and identified as law by certain master rules intrinsic to the system,[13] believe that in such a case no valid law exists. In rendering a decision the judge in fact functions as a legislator, albeit an "interstitial" one,[14] creating new law on the basis of utility, social policy, or other extralegal considerations. The judge is endowed by the legal system with the discretion to construct new legal norms which, filling the lacunae in the existing law, will serve as positive law to guide the decisions of future courts. This position has been attacked by Ronald Dworkin, who argues for a theory of "integrity in law".[15] Rejecting positivism's sharp distinction between law and morals, Dworkin contends that law cannot be reduced to a system of politically-enacted rules. Law contains principles as well, notions of justice and right which determine the judge's decision in cases where no explicit or sufficient rule exists. There is almost always a "right answer" to a hard case, dictated by the judge's conception of the most persuasive justification of the political morality of the legal system. The judge, in other words, does not enjoy the discretion to make new law, nor may he operate, as the legislator does, by ruling in accordance with his view of the best social policy. He interprets the law, deriving an answer for his hard case by constructing a theory which, in his view, is the most coherent account of the legal "data" (constitution, statutes, judicial precedents) with which he works. Since judges will disagree over these theories, they will disagree as to the "right answer"; that such an answer exists, however, is clear. It is an answer consistent with the fundamental principles of the law, not created by resort to considerations outside the law.[16] A third approach, denoted variously as "legal realism" or "rule-skepticism", tends to minimize the binding character of legal rules altogether. The law "is" as it is applied in practice, by courts and other adjudicatory bodies; rules, by contrast, are purely theoretical until enforced by such agencies. In its extreme expressions, legal realism denies that rules limit the discretion of the judge in any significant way, even in so-called "easy" cases. Rules are fictions, serving as a smokescreen of legal argumentation disguising the true motivations--social, psychological, political--of the judge.[17] Legal reasoning does not account for the decision. It reflects at best a "logic of exposition", an institutional requirement that judges explain their rulings to the community.[18] That judges accompany their rulings with reasoned opinions should not, however, blind us to the fact that a judicial decision is an act of legislation, a choice prompted by "extra-legal" factors, rather than of interpretation.

These schools of thought in secular jurisprudence bear a more-than-passing connection to our topic. As in other fields of research, scholars of Jewish law may attain a better understanding of their subject matter through the use of methodological tools developed for the analysis of similar, non-Jewish literary genres. We should be wary, of course, of drawing improper analogies. The theories of jurisprudence to which I refer were formulated to describe the workings of secular (primarily Anglo-Saxon) legal systems; their basic presumptions, accordingly, may not fit the realities of the *halakhic* process. Religious law, for one thing, does not make a sharp distinction between legal and moral norms in judicial reasoning.[19] In Jewish law, moreover, which lacks a recognized legislature, it may be as legitimate for the rabbinic decisor (*poseq*) to base his rulings upon policy considerations as upon strict rules of law.[20] Still, recent years have seen an increasing number of studies which examine Jewish law from the vantage point of the positivist/Dworkinian/realist debate.[21] For example, Haninah Ben-Menahem argues that during the *Talmudic* period the distinction between legal and extra-legal considerations was often ignored. *Talmudic* law was a system "governed by men, not by rules", tolerant of judicial deviation from the law in the interests of justice. Judges allowed themselves the authority to base their decisions upon extralegal factors and to set aside existing law without being authorized by the law itself to do so.[22] This pragmatic jurisprudence, law consciously employed to serve recognized social ends, is an extreme version of the realist approach.[23] Indeed, if Ben-Menahem is correct, the rabbis at this early stage of *halakhic* history did not feel compelled to restrict their frankly legislative activity to filling gaps in the law or to hide it behind a "smokescreen" of legal reasoning. Such judicial openness and flexibility, it would seem, is no longer present in rabbinic decision-making, and has been absent for a very long time. What is true of a legal system at its formative stage does not necessarily describe the same system at its later, more sophisticated (*i.e.*, formal) state.[24] Although liberal *halakhic* theorists tend to portray Jewish law as a dynamic, constantly-changing system which places an emphasis upon rabbinic freedom of decision, fifteen centuries of commentary and codification have had their say. The *poseq*, the rabbinic decisor, is no longer empowered to enforce justice at the expense of law. He is expected to operate within the framework of the *halakhah*, which is largely determined by the evolving consensus view held by the community of *posqim* past and present.[25] The *halakhic* tradition, reflected in its voluminous literature has in effect settled many questions that were formerly open, and rabbinic discretion to deviate from these settled points has correspondingly declined.

On the other hand, there still exist hard cases in *halakhah*. Issues arise over which there is no general agreement among the *posqim* as to the correct legal answer. More than that rabbis at times are in dispute over questions which at first glance do have such an answer, explicitly stated in the codes and ratified by generations of consensus.[26] Ours is such a hard case. Despite the unambiguous rulings of the *Mishneh Torah* and *Shulhan Arukh*, some rabbinic authorities permit the acceptance of converts who come to us out of clearly ulterior motives. Conversely, despite the authoritative gloss which leaves the final decision in the hands of the individual *Bet Din*, some authorities deny that rabbis are entitled ever to employ this grant of discretion. The question at hand is thus excellent material for a study of the nature of disagreement in the *halakhah*.

This essay is intended as a first step toward that study. I do not pretend to offer an exhaustive analysis of the legal issues involved, especially since others have worked this field.[27] I simply wish to examine the rabbinic disagreement over the issue from the perspective of theoretical jurisprudence. Does the dispute stem from the fact that, as the positivists would have it, there is no one "correct" answer and that the rabbis, like it or not, are constrained to create new law to fill the gap? Do we say, with Dworkin, that a correct answer exists and that the rabbis are arguing over interpretation rather than seeking to legislate according to extra-legal considerations? Or do we follow the realists and conclude that what appears to be *halakhic* argumentation simply masks the policy choices which are the ultimate cause of the rulings the *poskim* hand down? The Conclusion, in addition to a summary of the findings, will offer some comments as to the application of this kind of study in our efforts at delineating liberal *halakhah*.

I. Maimonides: Extreme Pragmatism and Its Discontents

A questioner poses the following case to the Rambam. A young man has scandalized his family by engaging in sexual relations with a Gentile maidservant he has purchased. Should the rabbinic court forcibly separate them, or does the principle of the law of *yefat to'ar* (Deut. 21:10-17 and *Qiddushin* 21b), where a ritual prohibition is relaxed in a situation where it is likely to be violated, apply in this case? In his brief and to-the-point response,[28] Rambam agrees that the law of the Torah requires a separation. The permit of the *yefat to'ar* is understood as a concession to human weakness, a step the law takes unwillingly; on the contrary, the *bet din* must employ every means at its disposal to force the man to expel the maidservant "or to free her and marry her". Rabbinic law, moreover, adds another stringency: A man suspected of a sexual liason with a maidservant or a Gentile woman is forbidden to marry her upon her conversion, although the marriage is valid should it take place. This is the existing law, the explicit rule of the *Mishnah* codified by Maimonides himself.[29] Yet in actual practice he sets aside the prohibition and allows the conversion and marriage.

> "When I have ruled in matters such as this that he expel her [*i.e.*, liberate her] and marry her, I have done so as a means of encouraging sinners to repent [*mipnei taqanat hashavim*], saying 'it is better that they eat the sauce and not the forbidden fat', relying upon the rabbinic principle that 'when it is time to act for the Lord, we must annul the Torah if necessary' (*M. Berakhot* 9:5, after Psalms 119:126). He is therefore permitted to marry her. May God in His mercy grant atonement for our sins, as He promised us: 'I will purge all your impurities' [Isaiah 1:25].

Rambam, in other words, deviates from the established law in two respects: he allows a conversion which is clearly not undertaken *leshem shamayim*,[30] and he permits the newly-converted maidservant to marry a man to whom she is expressly, if only *lekhat-hilah*, forbidden. Recognizing this deviation, he seeks to justify it, but his arguments, from a legal standpoint, are curiously weak. It is true, for example, that by waiving the "lesser" rabbinic decree against the conversion and marriage of this woman

(=sauce) Rambam saves the man from violating the "weightier" Toraitic prohibition against cohabitation with Gentiles (=forbidden fat).[31] It is also true that, in their well-known *taqanat hashavim*, the tannaitic sages pursued this "lesser of two evils" line by allowing a thief in certain cases to make monetary restitution rather than forcing him to meet the Toraitic requirement that he restore the actual stolen property.[32] This serves him as an implied *kal vahomer*: if the law of the Torah may be set aside in order to encourage repentance, such is certainly the case with the rabbinic prohibition against this marriage. The problem, as Rambam himself remarks concerning the Torah's indulgence of the evil impulse on the issue of *yefat to'ar*, is that this reasoning has no objective weight in Jewish law. The approach embodied in the *taqanat hashavim* was indeed utilized occasionally in the past and Rambam may deem it appropriate here,[33] but it has never been condoned as routine procedure. If the rabbis overruled a legal standard in this specific instance, they did not do so in other instances where the law was just as likely to be violated.[34] Some authorities have even criticized the "sauce rather than fat" argument as a dangerous notion, since if followed to its logical extreme it would sanction the annulment of any and all *mitzvot* in situations where lawless individuals threaten to violate them.[35]

The citation of "time to act for the Lord", while dramatic, raises similar difficulties. On its face, the principle allows the rabbinic authorities to ignore a specific *halakhic* standard in order to avert a calamity to the *halakhic* system as a whole. Yet how does one determine precisely that this is such a time to act? That determination, like the determination to employ *taqanat hashavim*, is inescapably subjective, so that two authorities confronting an identical situation might well draw diametrically opposite conclusions as to the proper course to take. Consider the decision of R. Shelomo b. Adret (Rashba, d. 1310) on virtually the same question as that which faces Rambam here.[36] A man buys a Gentile maidservant, cohabits with her, converts her to Judaism before she gives birth and keeps her in his house. Rashba condemns what he sees as an act of unacceptable lewdness. Citing the *Mishnaic* prohibition against this marriage, he declares that in his own community "no one...even the most vile and base, would behave in such an arrogant fashion, to dally with a maidservant, convert her and marry her". It is inconceivable to him that the local authorities would permit the violation of the *Mishnaic* rule, especially since "it is probable that she did not convert *leshem shamayim* but only to marry him." Rashba seems not to have known of Rambam's ruling, and it is impossible to tell whether such knowledge would have influenced his decision. What is certain is that, where Maimonides is concerned that the sinner be aided in returning to the path of righteousness and so determines to deviate from the law, Rashba's goal is to strengthen the standards of community morality by insisting that the law be enforced to its fullest extent. None of this, of course, proves that either of these two sages was "right" or "wrong" in his ruling. It does indicate, however, that Rambam's deviation from the law was not required by the law itself. He could just as legitimately have concluded, as did Rashba, that the rabbinic prohibition against the conversion and marriage must be upheld. Rambam's decision, that is, is very much his *decision*. His ruling is a conscious choice, an act of rabbinic will.

Nothing in the *halakhah*, no preexisting legal norm forces the Rambam to arrive at his decision to deviate from the law. The ruling is valid because, in Rambam's view, he has the power to make it; the *poseq* may choose to overrule existing law when "it is time to act for the Lord". While Psalms 119:126 is applied in the *Mishnah* to the specific issue of rendering the Oral Torah in writing, the rabbis in general are said to have the power to set aside Biblical commandments on a temporary basis "in order to restore the multitude to religion...just as a physician may amputate a hand or a foot in order to save the patient's life".[37] *Posqim*, therefore, need not always follow the law. They may go beyond the law, even negate it, when in their very subjective judgement the situation calls for that action.

    This is the language of extreme pragmatism, of the variety which Ben-Menahem claims was exercised by the *Talmudic* rabbis. Law must be applied so as to achieve the recognized political, moral, and social goals of the community. When existing law clashes with those goals, the judge may adjust or set aside the law. As the dispute between Rambam and Rashba attests, reasonable judges may disagree as to whether this is truly a "time to act for the Lord", whether the law ought to be set aside in a particular case. In the pragmatic view, however, that determination lies entirely with the judge, in his own evaluation of the needs of the hour. He is not restricted to judicial-style interpretation of settled law; he is endowed with the power of choice, the discretion to create new law and annul the old. In exercising this broad grant of discretionary power, the pragmatic judge thus functions openly as a legislator, and not necessarily an "interstitial" one.

    Rambam's pragmatism in dealing with this question constitutes a major exception to the rule described above, namely that rabbis no longer see themselves entitled, in this post-*Talmudic* age, to deviate from accepted and settled law as a means of securing the law's "higher" purposes. Were this exception to become the rule, it could serve as the foundation of a kind of pragmatic *halakhic* jurisprudence, in which rabbinic authorities would consciously and explicitly direct their decisions according to those purposes. The sources contain a good deal of material which supports this approach to halakhic decision. Dicta such as "you shall do what is just and good" (Deut. 6:18), "the court may coerce individuals not to act in the manner of Sodom", "its ways are ways of pleasantness" (Prov. 3:17), and "he is exempt from culpability under human law but liable under divine law" are occasionally cited in *Talmudic* literature to explain legal decisions which deviate from what is considered the fixed standard of the law.[38] One could make a case, based upon a strong interpretation of these principles, that Jewish law recognizes an equity jurisdiction similar to that which existed at one time alongside the English common law and within, though not separate from, the Roman law.[39] The same rabbis who are empowered to apply the rules of the formal *halakhah* are likewise entitled to judge cases according to other, more fluid principles of general justice when in their view the established law would produce an unfair or socially undesirable result. This explanation would account for the decision of Maimonides in our case, and it would clearly fit the theory and practice of *halakhah* in liberal Jewish circles.[40] As suggested above, however, it does not correspond to the behavior of the vast majority of *halakhists* since the close of the *Talmudic* period, who do not, as a rule, feel authorized to deviate from the settled law on the basis of such principles as "time to act for the Lord".[41] Historical, theological, and jurisprudential explanations for this trend vary and abound.[42] For our purposes it is enough to stress that it *is* the centuries-old *tendency* in Jewish law, a rule proven by Rambam's striking and all too rare exception.

With respect to our subject, post-*Talmudic halakhists* might well agree that, for reasons of community policy, it is better in some cases to permit conversions that are undertaken for ulterior motives. And some leading rabbinic scholars of the past two centuries have made that ruling. Where they differ from Rambam is that, lacking Maimonidean levels of self-confidence, most (though not all) are loathe to deviate openly from the accepted legal norm. Their task is to demonstrate that, contrary to first impressions, no such deviation is involved, that the established law in fact allows these conversions.

II. Kluger, Hoffmann, Grodzinsky: Positivism in the Service of Leniency

The problem of conversion for ulterior motives has become a much more pressing issue for *halakhists* during the past two centuries, as emancipation has brought Jews into the life of their surrounding communities and secularization has softened the taboos against social contact with Gentiles. The *posqim* have had to deal with an increasing number of Jews wishing to marry Gentiles, a phenomenon complicated by the fact that, should the rabbis refuse to allow the conversion of the non-Jewish marriage partner, the couple can turn to other sources of relief: liberal rabbis, civil marriage, and even non-Jewish religious marriage. For a number of these rabbis, the availability of non-*halakhic* marriage serves not only as a threat to communal discipline but also as an argument that the prohibition against conversion in these cases may no longer apply.

R. Shelomo Kluger (d. 1869), a leading Lithuanian respondent, is asked for his opinion on a case which has arisen in "the lands of Germany and France, where the new religion has taken hold".[43] A Jewish man has fallen in love with a Gentile woman "and cohabited with her several times". He has now returned to the Jewish community, and "it is her intention to convert to Judaism". Kluger permits the conversion. Relying upon the sources cited at the beginning of this essay, he notes that while those who convert for the purpose of marriage are not to be accepted, the *Bet Din* has the discretion to determine in any particular case whether the prospective convert has come to us *leshem shamayim*. In our case, that determination can be made for two reasons. First, since the Jew has cohabited with his lover "many"[44] times, we can presume that his desire to marry her is not founded upon lust (or, in the more elegant *Talmudic* phrase, *leshem ishah*, for the sake of marrying this woman). Second, it is clear that this man is of an impulsive disposition (*da'ato kalah*). He stands on the brink of apostasy (*qarov lehishtamed*); should we refuse our permission, he will convert to his lover's religion and marry her anyway. Since he has *not* done this, therefore, since the couple have "returned to his father's house", we have evidence that "her intention is to convert *leshem shamayim* and not for the purpose of marriage." A major obstacle to this decision exists, however, in *M. Yevamot* 2:8, which declares that a man suspected of a sexual relationship with a Gentile woman is not permitted to marry her should she convert to Judaism. At first, Kluger suggests that this prohibition be read quite strictly, so that it apply only to cases in which the liason was "suspected" but not a known fact. Since the stated reason for the prohibition is to avoid public slander, one could argue that when slander cannot be avoided (*i.e.*, when the affair is common knowledge) the prohibition ought to be waived. He retreats from this argument, however. Other sources do apply the prohibition to cases where it is known with certainty that the couple have cohabited.[45] Moreover, he continues, to say that the marriage is permitted when we know for a certainty that the Jew has committed this transgression (and not if we are in doubt as to whether he did it) is the kind of reasoning that can make a mockery of the rabbinic law. Rather, Kluger points to the fact that if we refuse our permission the man will become an apostate. We can allow the conversion and marriage, he says, in order to prevent this terrible result, much as Isserles has ruled that a man suspected of a liason with an unmarried woman, though forbidden *lehat-hilah* to marry her, may do so in order to prevent her from falling into bad company (*tarbut ra'ah*).[46]

Kluger's permissive conclusion parallels that of Rambam: both allow a conversion and marriage which apparently violate the established law. The emphasis, however, must be placed upon "apparently". While his illustrious predecessor admits that his decision deviates from the law and justifies that deviation by resort to overriding concerns of religious and community policy, Kluger recognizes no such transgression. The conversion and marriage are perfectly "legal", their validity "declared" by the established law itself through the process of interpretation and not "created" through an act of the *poseq*'s will. Extralegal factors-for example, an analysis of whether a permissive ruling is good or bad for the community or whether the behavior of this couple undermine the standards of Jewish religious life-are conspicuous by their absence. Kluger presents himself as the oracle of the *halakhah* and not its legislator; he arrives at his decision not by making new law but by applying the canons of textual logic so that the sources might yield up the correct answer already contained within.

A closer look, though, reveals that Kluger's ruling depends upon a daring exercise of rabbinic discretion which, though concealed beneath the surface, compares well to that which the Rambam employs openly. Consider the manner in which he determines that this conversion is undertaken "for the sake of Heaven". Even if we do not define the concept, as some do, as an exalted, virtually unattainable level of religious purity,[47] the requirement that a convert come to Judaism *leshem shamayim* would surely seem to require positive evidence of his or her religious sincerity. Kluger stands this presumption on its head. A decision to convert can be judged as *leshem shamayim* in the absence of positive evidence to the contrary, that is, that the individual desires conversion in order to obtain some temporal object or goal. In our case, the woman need not convert in order to cohabit with her Jewish lover, since they will remain together in any event. In this strictly formal sense, the conversion is not contemplated for the ulterior motivation of marriage (*leshem ishut*); by process of elimination, therefore, we may conclude that the motivation for the conversion is religiously sincere.

The problem with this designation is two-fold. On the level of fact, the fit is unpersuasive. We have here a clearly non-observant Jew who is quite prepared to embrace another religion if necessary in order to marry a Gentile woman, whose attachment to Judaism can hardly be any deeper than that of her prospective husband.[48] It is one thing to say that, technically, this couple do not need the cooperation of the *Bet Din* in order to marry. To conclude that their motivation is *leshem shamayim*-and Kluger explicitly applies that label to them - is precisely the kind of sophistry which Kluger himself condemns in his discussion of *M. Yevamot* 2:8. On the level of law, even if "sincerity" is equated with the absence of a formal ulterior motive, Kluger relies upon an unnecessarily strict-constructionist definition of that term. This point is brought out by R. Meir Arik who, facing a similar case, makes a forceful critique of Kluger's reasoning.[49] The meaning of "ulterior motive" *ilah*, in the language of the codes)[50] is not exhausted by the stated examples, such as "for the sake of marriage". The category, says Arik, includes "any kind of pretext", and in our case, "perhaps the man now wants to live with her in honor and not in a licentious manner (*behefqerut*)". The couple do not require a conversion in order to live together, but they do need it in order to live together legitimately within the Jewish community. That desire, while it may be laudable, does not prove that the woman wants to become a Jew for the purpose of serving God as a member of the covenant people of Israel.

Kluger, by contrast, defines "ulterior motive" more narrowly and, as the obverse side of the coin, "for the sake of Heaven" more broadly than does Arik. The issue here is not whether he, as opposed to Arik, has the better argument. As I have indicated, Kluger's definitions of "ulterior motive" and "sincerity" do seem to run afoul of the canons of plausibility and common sense, but the lay understanding of terminology is not always decisive in the technical world of law and *halakhah*. It is rather that his making of that argument is an act of choice, of rabbinic discretion. Nothing in the *halakhic* texts forces him to define these crucial terms as he does. Were he to choose the opposite set of definitions, those favored by Arik, he would have no choice but to conclude that the conversion is forbidden by *halakhah*. To permit it, he would have to emulate Rambam and set aside the established law in favor of some overriding principle. His own set of definitions allows him to champion the conversion as perfectly "legal"; no deviation is necessary. My point is simply that this conclusion, presented as a logical inference demanded by the words of the texts, is not that at all. It is a *choice* which Kluger makes between two legitimate alternatives.

The difficulties with that choice can be seen in the ruling of R. David Zvi Hoffmann (Germany, d. 1921), who cites Kluger's *hidush* (though not the responsum itself) as the basis for his permissive decisions in two cases where Jews are either married to Gentiles according to civil law or contemplating such marriage.[51] Since the conversions sought in these instances are not technically for the sake of marriage, we may allow them. Yet at the same time, Hoffmann cannot regard the prospective conversions as evidence of religious sincerity; "how can the *Bet Din* accept a proselyte who does not convert *leshem shamayim*?" Unlike Kluger, therefore, Hoffmann turns outside the established law, supporting his decision with arguments of principle and policy. For his principle, he relies upon II Samuel 24:17 ("and these sheep, how have they sinned?"), stressing that the future children of these couples ought not to suffer for the misdeeds of their parents. As his policy consideration, he notes that should we refuse the conversion, the non-Jewish partner will be converted by a liberal rabbi. This will produce unfortunate consequences, since the public will then consider that partner a Jew even though liberal conversions are invalid under *halakhah*. Thus, "it is better to seize the lesser of two evils" and permit the conversion.[52]

Hoffmann's approach nicely illustrates the difference between "legal" and "extralegal" arguments in a responsum. Legal arguments are based upon rules whose applicability to the case at hand is unquestioned and which are subject to demonstration by means of textual analysis, even if that analysis does not persuade other scholars. Extralegal arguments are by their nature controversial; they cannot be "proven", merely advocated. Their applicability to the case at hand is likewise controversial.[53] For example, in a similar case R. Chaim Ozer Grodzinsky (Lithuania, d. 1940)[54] rejects out of hand his correspondent's concern that should the *Bet Din* turn him away the prospective convert will go to a Reform rabbi. "We cannot worry about this...a proper *Bet Din* must act strictly according to *halakhic* procedures" and not violate them in order to save an individual (the Jewish spouse) from committing a sin. Citing Rambam's decision, he notes that the issue there concerns the owner of the Gentile maidservant, who can convert her upon his own authority, and not the religious court. If an individual may transgress the law in order to save himself from a greater sin, this does not mean that the *Bet Din*, which represents the rule of law in the community, is so entitled. Besides, the "lesser of two evils" argument, which plays such an important role for Rambam, Kluger, and Hoffmann, does not really fit our case. Grodzinsky points out that if we allow the conversion of a Gentile wife, her husband will thereupon become a transgressor of the commandment against sexual intercourse with a *niddah*, a rule which does not apply to Gentile women. That transgression, punishable by *karet*,[55] is a more serious one than that of cohabiting with a Gentile, which does not carry that harsh punishment; we are not, therefore, "saving" a Jew from sin by permitting the conversion. In other words, Grodzinsky concludes, none of these extralegal considerations justifies the conversion. It *can* be permitted because, since it is not undertaken "for the sake of marriage", there is no *halakhic* barrier to it, even if it is not good policy for the Jews in general or for this Jew in particular.

Ultimately, for these lenient authorities, conversion for the sake of marriage can be allowed only on the basis of the legal argument formulated by R. Shelomo Kluger. In this they differ from Rambam, whose similar ruling is presented as a conscious deviation from settled *halakhah*. By reasoning that such conversions do not technically fall under the rubric of *leshem ishut*, they expand the boundaries of the permissible in Jewish law, allowing it to include a phenomenon which clearly would not fit within previous conceptions of those boundaries. That "reasoning", however, that close adherence to purely legal argumentation, should not blind us to the fact that these authorities have *chosen* to read the law as they have. The motivation for their choice might lie, as it clearly does for Hoffmann, in an estimate of policy, of what is best for the Jewish community in this particular situation. Kluger and Grodzinsky make no such claim; they do, nonetheless, make a choice. In this, they confirm the positivist model: judges facing "hard cases" answer them through the exercise of discretionary, virtually legislative power, even when their choices are expressed through the medium of conventional legal argumentation.

III. Kook and Herzog: Principles and Interpretation

Those willing to permit conversion for the sake of marriage rely upon the premise that the conversion, even if prohibited by rabbinic enactment, is Toraitically valid (*bedi'avad*) should it take place. This premise is challenged in decisions issued by two chief rabbis of Palestine/Israel, R. Avraham Yitzhaq Hakohen Kook[56] and R. Yitzhaq Halevy Herzog.[57] A good argument can be made for the invalidity of these conversions, even though the notion is a minority opinion.[58] The argument is Dworkinian in nature: it answers a "hard case" according to that theory which in the judge's view is the most coherent account of the legal "data" on the subject, regardless of the consequentialist (=policy) implications of that answer.

Kook addresses a responsum to R. Shaul Setton, one of the authors of a 1927 rabbinic decree banning conversion in Argentina.[59] Kook thinks the ban is a good idea and supports it by showing that the "data" of Jewish law overwhelmingly oppose the acceptance of religiously insincere converts.[60] Indeed, as we learn in *Bekhorot* 30b, "one who accepts the entire Torah with the exception of the tiniest detail is not allowed to convert". This position is held universally in the *halakhic* world, says Kook, who is therefore puzzled that the great codes omit this statement entirely. This is reminiscent of Dworkin's "theory of mistakes": when a judge finds that his best available interpretation of the law cannot account for certain "data" of legal history, he has no choice but to declare those data to be mistaken, contradicted by the preponderance of the precedents upon which he relies.[61] The failure of Maimonides and Karo to codify the rule of *Bekhorot* 30b, a silence that deviates from the tradition's consistent emphasis that the proselyte accept the Torah in its entirety, is such a mistake, and it therefore does not constitute evidence that the rule itself is not authoritative. And since, as far as Kook is concerned, the vast majority of converts today do not accept the Torah unconditionally and in its entirety, a ban on conversions has powerful *halakhic* justification.

This interpretation of the law similarly allows Kook to address another "hard case": when an insincere proselyte undergoes the conversion ritual, is his conversion a valid one? Again, the "data" are conflicting. On the one hand, the codes rule that once a person undergoes the ritual, even if he does so for ulterior motives, "he is a convert". That is to say, the ritual brings about an automatic change in the person's legal status, regardless of the intentions he brought with him to that moment. On the other hand, those same rulings add a proviso concerning this person: "we watch him carefully until his sincerity is proven", suggesting that insincere intent might render the rituals ineffective.[62] Kook resolves this contradiction of rules as follows: the conversion of an insincere proselyte is valid ("he is a convert") only when subsequent investigation ("we watch him carefully") reveals that his conversion was "complete", that is, accompanied by observance of the *mitzvot*. When both factors, religious sincerity and religious observance, are absent (as they are clearly absent in the vast majority of cases of conversion for the sake of marriage), we conclude that regardless of the ritual no real conversion ever took place.[63] For this reason such persons should never be permitted to convert and, should they convert, should never be permitted to marry Jews.

In his resolution of this legal ambiguity, Kook aims at *coherence*, or what Dworkin refers to as "integrity in law". To account for the full range of rulings and statements on conversion in the *halakhic* literature, he develops a general interpretive theory of the *halakhah* on the subject, which in turn allows him to distinguish between possible answers to his "hard case", the ambiguous wording of the codes. One possible answer, that insincere conversions are nonetheless valid, contradicts his interpretation of the *halakhah*, which makes a consistent demand that the convert display religious sincerity. The other possible answer, which limits this validity to cases where the conversion is ratified by subsequent religious observance, is more coherent, a better fit with his interpretive theory, minimizing contradictions and maximizing legal consistency. In approaching the case in this way, Kook marches in lock step with Dworkin's conception of a good judge.

Herzog fully endorses Kook's position. Throughout his responsa on our issue, he argues that the majority *halakhic* position, which declares that insincere conversions are valid *bedi'avad*, is no longer applicable. His particular contribution on this point is his citation of those *rishonim* who justify the validity of insincere conversions only when subsequently ratified by observance of the *mitzvot*.[64] In this, he provides concrete theoretical backing to Kook's logical inference to the same effect. This ruling, in turn, provokes another "hard case": if we say that insincere conversions are invalid, must we not therefore declare that the marriages which followed them are likewise invalid? This conclusion follows logically from its premise, yet other "data" in the law contradict it. Most notable among these is the very rule against which Herzog and Kook argue, namely that insincere conversions are accepted as valid once they take place. Although Herzog, as we have seen, does not believe that this rule applies today, he admits that his and Kook's position may not be the correct one; others, that is, would dispute it. Since there is doubt as to the correct *halakhah* (*i.e.*, since there is no dominant consensus view among *halakhists*) we must resort to the principle *sofeiqa de'oraita lehumra*, doubt in matters of Toraitic law requires us to rule stringently. In this case, the stringent ruling would hold the marriages valid (*i.e.*, a *get* would be necessary to dissolve them). In this way Herzog avoids the potentially devastating consequences which Kook's opinion, if accepted, would exert upon Jewish communal stability, Jewish identity and the like. Yet it should be noted that he does not mention these consequences as the justification for his ruling. Like Kook, Herzog approaches his "hard cases" as a Dworkinian. His argumentation rests upon principle, not policy. His conclusion is supported by means of legal reasoning, by tools internal to Jewish law which come into play to resolve issues of doubt, rather than by the extralegal concern over what effect a different decision would have upon the community.[65]

For all their devotion to matters internal to law, Kook and Herzog nonetheless exercise wide discretion in rendering their decisions. The key to this discretion can be found in Herzog's acknowledgement that, while conversion for the sake of marriage is certainly prohibited and very possibly invalid should it take place, some *halakhic* precedents allow them (he cites Rambam and Kluger) and some communities accept proselytes in these cases. Kook, who is obviously aware of these facts of precedent and practice, ignores them completely, a studied ignorance which enables him to issue his unequivocal condemnation. Herzog, on the other hand, takes judicial notice of these facts, which serve as the basis for an alternative interpretation of the *halakhah*. If he is not persuaded by that interpretation, he at least recognizes its existence as a legitimate (if inferior) understanding of the law. He therefore has grounds to accept, if grudgingly, the custom of some rabbinic courts to permit conversions in situations where he personally would not. In the end, he leaves it to the discretion (*shiqul da'at*) of the local rabbi to determine whether in each individual case the proselyte meets the *halakhic* requirement of religious sincerity and whether he or she will likely observe the commandments. Thus Herzog, while agreeing with Kook in theory, is much more flexible on the issue of these conversions in practice. The difference is the result of discretion: Herzog is no more forced to cite the alternative precedents and practices than is Kook forced to omit any mention of them. Both of them *choose* to cite or to ignore the data, and their choices determine their final rulings.

IV. Moshe Feinstein: The *Poseq* as Realist

Herzog gives us an example of what we might call the "alternative theory" in *halakhic* decision-making. A *poseq* declares the *halakhah* according to his best understanding of it and at the same time seeks to explain the reasoning behind the contrary or opposite ruling, even though he himself rejects that reasoning. As his example shows, this is no mere act of intellectual courtesy. Practical legal consequences stem from the existence of an alternative theory, in much the same way as a minority opinion, though rejected, carries concrete *halakhic* implications.[66] A similar illustration emerges from two of the rulings of R. Moshe Feinstein on our subject.[67]

The first of these deals with a Jewish man who married his Gentile spouse in a civil ceremony; the couple have lived together for a number of years, and they have a son. Feinstein declares that there is no rabbinic impediment to a Jewish marriage in this instance. Contrary to R. Shelomo Kluger, he limits the prohibition in *M. Yevamot* 2:8 to a man suspected of a liason with a Gentile woman and excludes the man who has lived openly in a marital relationship with her. There is, however, a Toraitic impediment: the woman needs to become a Jew, and conversion in such a case is forbidden. On this issue, too, Feinstein parts company with Kluger. He suggests, as does R. Meir Arik, that while this couple do not require a conversion in order to live together as husband and wife, "there may be some other ulterior motive [*sibah*] that impels her to convert. And since she is converting only on account of that motive, it is probable that she does not intend to accept the commandments of the Torah." Feinstein, in other words, does not accept Kluger's strict construction of "ulterior motive" which allows the latter to define a conversion of this sort as *leshem shamayim*. He strengthens the point by noting that we can hardly expect this woman upon her conversion to be more observant than her husband, a violator of (among others) the laws of *Shabbat* and *nidah*. Since most contemporary conversions fall into this category, "most rabbis who are true scholars and fearers of Heaven" refuse to handle conversions at all. Still, community political pressure may make it impossible for the rabbi (Feinstein's correspondent) to refuse to convert this woman. If so, then he should do his best. He should explain very carefully to her the requirements of Judaism and obtain her promise to uphold them, regardless of her husband's irreligious behavior. "Perhaps (this promise) can be considered acceptance of the *mitzvot*, so that, although this conversion should not be allowed *lehat-hilah*...it is still a valid conversion." This "perhaps" serves as a *halakhic* justification, albeit a weak one, for a decision which the local rabbi most likely cannot avoid.

In the second case, Feinstein's correspondent asks whether a woman converted by a Conservative rabbi may be buried in the communal cemetery. Not surprisingly, Feinstein rejects any hint of validity in the non-Orthodox conversion ceremony, since there can be no legitimate *qabalat hamitzvot* (acceptance of the commandments) before a *Bet Din* whose members by his definition "deny many central tenets of Judaism and violate a number of ritual prohibitions".[68] Even worse from his perspective is the fact that some Orthodox rabbis accept proselytes who want to marry Jews and who clearly do not intend to observe the commandments. As in the previous case, however, Feinstein seeks to defend these rabbis by providing a *halakhic* explanation for their practice. He suggests, first of all, that the *Bet Din* may be entitled to accept the convert's declaration that he or she will uphold the Torah. Even though most converts in our day have no such intention, some actually mean it, and because of these few we might give the others the benefit of the doubt. Additionally, it is possible that their intentions, while misguided, are sincere. That is, the convert probably thinks that "to accept the commandments" really means "to behave as a Jew ought to behave", and this he is prepared to do. Of course, the Jews in the community, and certainly those in the convert's immediate environment, violate the commandments, and he will think that their actions constitute a truly Jewish religious lifestyle. This is an error, of course, but one due to his innocent ignorance, and ignorance of the commandments is not a fatal flaw in the conversion process.[69] It is only when the proselyte is aware of the commandments and positively intends *not* to observe them that the conversion may be rendered invalid. Since this convert has no such positive intention, he has in principle accepted the obligation to observe the *mitzvot*, even if in fact he will violate them afterwards. "This," Feinstein concludes, "is a limited justification (*limud zekhut ketzat*) for those rabbis who accept such converts, so that they (the rabbis) will not be thought of as worse than ignorant."

Limited indeed. Feinstein clearly does not swallow the explanations he has created to justify rabbinic acceptance of conversion for the sake of marriage. He personally sides with those "scholars and fearers of Heaven" who refuse to involve themselves with conversions, since it is evident to all (*anan sahadei*) that the vast majority of proselytes in our day do not accept upon themselves the obligation to observe the *mitzvot*. Nonetheless, his alternative theories play a crucial role in his understanding of the halakhic system and its practice, a role that thinkers of the legal realist camp can readily appreciate. A cornerstone in realist doctrine is the assertion that the legal argumentation presented in judicial opinions often masks the policy considerations which actually account for the judge's ruling. It is not difficult to gauge the policy goals that drive Feinstein in these cases, particularly since his reasoning is meant to justify not his own decisions but those of other rabbis.[70] Consider that these responsa were directed to rabbis in small communities (the "outskirts of Pittsburgh" and Canton, Ohio, respectively) at a time (1952 and 1950) when American Orthodoxy, not having entered its current self-confident triumphalist phase, was struggling for survival. For their own professional survival, Orthodox rabbis frequently found it necessary to compromise their standards of observance in the face of community pressure. An outright condemnation of conversion for the sake of marriage, in the style of Rav Kook, would correspond to the "true", ideal *halakhah*, but it would place these rabbis and others like them in the unenviable position of having to deviate from normative Judaism in order to officiate, as they must, at such conversions. Feinstein elects a middle path. He recognizes on the one hand the correct theory of the law which forbids these conversions and regards them as invalid should they take place.[71] On the other hand, by straining to create his alternative theories, he allows these rabbis to maintain at least the appearance of *halakhic* integrity while taking actions which are forced upon them.

Like Herzog, Feinstein's alternative theory approach permits him a degree of legal flexibility that serves an important, practical purpose. We should, however, take note of the difference between these two authorities. Herzog's alternative theory is based upon an existing line of rabbinic precedents, decisions of respectable *posqim* whose prestige is unquestioned even though one may disagree with them. Feinstein, by contrast, seems not to accept these precedents at all and so must create his alternative theories out of thin air. The theories are thus excessively weak, and Feinstein himself shows them little respect. For him, this is not a case of legitimate *halakhic mahloqet*, an issue over which reasonable rabbinic scholars can disagree. The permissive position is in fact *wrong*, *un*reasonable, and exists only to provide halakhic cover for rabbis who in their hearts know better. It functions as Feinstein's version of the "lesser-of-two-evils" policy argument: it is better for rabbis to justify their decisions by means of patently weak *halakhic* argumentation than to deviate openly from the law. Like all policy arguments, this one can be challenged on the basis of the facts. Perhaps the opposite is true: resort to such *halakhic* sleight-of-hand may be the surest way to destroy the respect of the laity for the Jewish legal system. The point, however, is not whether or not Feinstein's policy judgement is correct but rather that he makes it. It is an act of his discretion, a *choice* which he makes to serve a purpose other than the determination of what, strictly speaking, is the authoritative *halakhah* in this case.

V. Benzion Uziel: A Return to Pragmatism

Feinstein's approach can be termed "pragmatic", although in a backhanded sort of way: his judgement of practical necessity leads him to devise a legal theory not to account for his own, presumably correct ruling but rather the incorrect rulings of other rabbis. A clearer example of *halakhic* pragmatism can be found in the opinions of R. Benzion Meir Hai Uziel, who served as the first Sephardic Chief Rabbi of Israel until his death in 1953. One decision, dating from his years as rabbi in Salonica, is especially interesting. Uziel permits the non-Jewish wife of a Jewish man (and, importantly, the mother of his children) to convert and marry him according to *halakhah*. In his responsum,[72] he cites the sources which prohibit conversion when undertaken for an ulterior motive, along with the gloss declaring that "the entire matter is left to the judgement of the court".[73] He suggests that in this case, discretion argues for permitting the conversion and marriage, on the grounds that

> "(the wife) will be drawn ever closer to her husband's family and religion. Moreover, her present and future children will be fully Jewish (*yehudim gemurim*). This is analogous to the cases of Hillel and R. Hiyya, who were certain that their converts would eventually become true proselytes. It is

therefore permitted, even commanded, to bring these people into the covenant of Israel and thereby expunge the blight of intermarriage that is now a raging pestilence..."

The cases, of course, are *not* so similar. Hillel and R. Hiyya were persuaded that their converts would eventually "do so *leshem shamayim*",[74] a term generally understood to imply the observance of the *mitzvot*. Here, Uziel provides absolutely no evidence that such an outcome is predictable. How "Jewish" will this woman ever be? How observant is her husband, whose religion she will eventually - after her conversion-come to accept? Uziel offers no discussion of this issue, nor does he claim, following Kluger *et al.*, that a conversion in a situation such as this is in fact *leshem shamayim*. Indeed, the religious sincerity of the prospective proselyte is virtually irrelevant to his decision. He permits the conversion, not because he can predict that the woman will eventually accept all the commandments, but because of the potentially negative consequences which would result from denying it. As he makes clear in a related responsum, Uziel radically expands the discretionary power granted by the phrase "the entire matter is left to the judgement of the court", holding that the rabbis may permit a conversion even if clearly undertaken for ulterior motives, since that course of action is necessary to combat the plague of intermarriage "that threatens to wreak destruction upon our people."[75] This is a dramatic departure from the codified *halakhah*, which is decidedly non-consequentialist: a conversion is permissible, not because to permit it is good for the Jews, but because the convert wishes to become a Jew "for the sake of Heaven". Uziel, alone among the *posqim* we have surveyed, makes the general welfare of the Jewish community the pivotal factor in deciding the *halakhah* on this issue.

His pragmatism shows itself as well in his treatment of the second issue in this case: if we allow this woman to convert, may she marry her current husband according to Jewish law? The rabbinic prohibition of such marriages (*M. Yevamot* 2:8) is an apparently insurmountable obstacle. Uziel surveys various legal devices that have over the years been suggested as ways to circumvent the prohibition, but he concludes that all of them are *halakhically* defective. Ultimately, we are left with one sure remedy: the responsum of Maimonides discussed above. Indeed, as his other responsa on this issue suggest, Rambam's ruling is the linchpin of Uziel's position on both issues, the conversion as well as the marriage.[76] It shows us that we may deviate from the settled law in the name of higher religious purpose. Uziel declares that Rambam's lesser-of-two-evils argument "serves as a guide on all matters which do not involve an absolute prohibition (*isur gamur*; i.e., rabbinic as opposed to Toraitic prohibitions)":[77] to avoid potentially tragic consequences to the Jewish people, the prohibition may be waived.

Uziel, in other words, uses Rambam as his precedent, which allows him to contend that he does not actually deviate from the law at all. If Maimonides, a post-*Talmudic* authority, can suspend *Talmudic* law on the basis of a "lesser-of-two-evils" argument, Uziel can do so as well. True, he does not *have* to do so, since Jewish law does not recognize a doctrine of binding precedent. The fact that a great authority ruled in a particular way on a question of *halakhah* does not obligate a subsequent scholar to rule likewise. The ultimate authority, after all, is the Babylonian *Talmud*, and the *halakhist's* responsibility is to decide questions according to his best understanding of the *Talmudic* sources regardless of the opinions of other *posqim*.[78] Still, a past decision may count as a "precedent" to the extent that it influences the thinking of a contemporary scholar. In theory, rabbis are free to arrive at their own independent decisions; in practice, they customarily cite the decisions of post-*Talmudic* predecessors in support of their own rulings. Even the eminent codifiers attribute decisive weight to precedent in their determination of the *halakhah*.[79] The opinions of past scholars do not automatically establish the *halakhah*, but they do serve a persuasive function, as evidence that the law, *in all probability*, is in accordance with their view. In our case, Uziel is on solid ground in basing his ruling upon that of the Rambam. Indeed, by hitching his wagon to a *halakhist* of towering prestige, he can claim that his lenient and seemingly radical decision is justified by the existing law. Its legitimacy, that is, does not depend solely upon his arbitrary act of discretion.

This point, however, does not save his decision from criticism. The problem here is not that Uziel relies on precedent but that he relies on *this* precedent instead of the available alternative, that of Rashba, who as we have seen took a stringent attitude on an almost identical set of facts. Uziel is aware of Rashba's ruling, and he cites it in his responsum. If, therefore, he wishes to argue from the law rather than from his own subjective judgement, how does he know that the law follows one version rather than another? What legal rule, that is, allows him to favor Rambam over Rashba? A Dworkinian approach would be to apply the test of coherence, giving the nod to that ruling which better conforms to the legal "data" and is endorsed by the preponderance of scholarly opinion. Ouziel takes the opposite tack. He does not attempt to prove that Rambam is "right"; it is enough that Rashba is also not necessarily "right". The law, that is to say, *might* be according to either position, giving Uziel an opening to adopt Rambam's view as the best means to preserve Jewish identity and to save the Jewish spouse from the prohibition of intermarriage. Ultimately, then, Ouziel's justification is consequentialist and not strictly legal: when the law is in dispute, we are entitled to choose that position which promises the better consequences for the community.[80]

Such, in brief, is the doctrine of legal pragmatism. Judges should opt for that legal alternative which best supports the ends which the law itself is intended to achieve. In our case, to hold to the accepted rule and deny conversion on the grounds that the Gentile wife does not have the proper religious motivations is to allow an intermarriage to continue to exist. To enforce the law is to weaken Jewish life, to lower its powers of resistance against the rising tide of assimilation. To relax the *halakhic* standards on conversion, on the other hand, would help save this couple and their children for Judaism. The reasoning is certainly compelling, but it may be wrong. For one thing, Rambam's lenient ruling may not be a legitimate potential interpretation of the *halakhah* in our case;[81] in situations such as this, the surest course of action is the more conservative approach (*i.e.*, following Rashba, to refrain from abetting an improper conversion and marriage). Moreover, assuming that all agree on the "end" to be achieved--here, to combat intermarriage--the stringent approach of Rashba is perhaps the best means of achieving it. A plausible argument can be made that in the face of widespread disregard of Jewish law the worst thing we can do is to relax the observance of halakhic standards. Such a tactic, which promises sinners a reward for their transgression, can hardly engender respect for the Torah and its commandments. To compromise on our devotion to the *mitzvot* may therefore weaken the intensity and quality of Jewish religious life--the very goals that Uziel seeks to attain. In other words, while Uziel follows the precedent of Rambam, the better policy may be that advocated by Rashba, who refused to allow conversion and marriage in a similar case. The determination of the "better policy" would seem to demand an empirical study based upon sociological and demographic data, yet Uziel cites no such data to support his preference for Rambam over Rashba. We return, therefore, to our question: on what *halakhic* basis are we entitled to follow Rambam as opposed to the other authorities?

Clearly, the only reason is that Uziel says so. The identification of Rambam as "the" authoritative precedent is an act of choice, a stated preference for one opinion over another, supported not by *halakhic* argumentation but by the *poseq*'s intuitive, fervently-held belief that this is the best thing for rabbis in this situation to do. In this he demonstrates a fundamental truth about the use of precedent in legal reasoning: judges may rely upon past decisions as authorities, but the determination of *which* decisions (and which aspects of those decisions) will serve as their precedents is a matter of discretion, "a choice as to what the precedent *shall* be."[82] The "law" does not compel Uziel to recognize Rambam's ruling as his precedent. In the final analysis, his *choice* to so recognize it is justified by his unprovable conviction that this is the best choice he can make and by the undeniable fact that, as a leading *poseq*, he has the power to make it. In Ouziel, therefore, we find one of those rare exceptions to the *halakhic* rule, a rabbi willing to countenance deviation from the established *halakhah* in order to realize the goals and purposes of Torah as a whole.

VI. Conclusion

To repeat, the intent of this essay was not to provide a comprehensive survey of the *halakhah* on conversion for the sake of marriage but rather to study some representative responsa on the subject using analytical tools developed by students of modern jurisprudence. The results, if tentative and sketchy, suggest the following conclusions (themselves tentative and sketchy; obviously, the topic deserves a much more extensive treatment than is possible here).

1. The application of these methodologies to the responsa literature is a promising field for future research. That vast literature has by no means been ignored by academic scholars, who have mined it for data on Jewish economic and social history, biographical material on the great respondents, details concerning religious currents and the like.[83] In doing so, however, they have necessarily ignored the responsum itself, as a genre of rabbinic writing, in favor of the information it happens to contain. They

have thus missed the purpose and point of responsa writing, which is to answer queries concerning theoretical and practical *halakhah*. Other academic scholars, studying the history of the development of Jewish law, have paid closer attention to the more purely *halakhic* aspects of the *sheelot uteshuvot*.[84] Yet they, too, in focusing their energies upon the responsum's *halakhic* "bottom line", have perforce had to overlook the document's essential nature as a *decision*, a literary reconstruction of the process by which a rabbinic scholar has drawn upon various sources in an attempt to reason from the known to the unknown. It just may be that the most interesting feature of a responsum is not the *poseq*'s final conclusion (the "holding", in judicial terminology) but the intellectual map which charts how he arrived at that destination. His reasoning and justification may well be that aspect of his responsum which exerts the most long-lasting influence upon future scholars. To analyze the responsa from this standpoint can yield us a better understanding of how the established *halakhah*, the law as expressed in the "codes" and through the consensus of rabbinic practitioners, came to be.

    2. The decisions examined in this essay use a variety of methods of arriving at answers to the "hard case" of conversion for the sake of marriage. These correspond to the theoretical models of judicial decision put forward by the leading thinkers in the academy of modern jurisprudence. Some of our *posqim* display an openly pragmatic bent, justifying their answers on the grounds that a better (or less evil) conclusion follows from a decision which frankly departs from the standards of settled law (Rambam, Uziel), though we have also seen that the weakness of this justification is that it rests not upon legal reasoning but upon the *poseq*'s subjective, unprovable value judgement (Rashba). Others, who reach the same permissive conclusion as the pragmatists, are unwilling to take the step of deviation from the settled *halakhah*, and they therefore must support their answer by means of a narrow reading of the positive law (Kluger). Some find it necessary to

buttress this approach by pointing to policy considerations that demand this ruling (Hoffmann); in this, we see an example of the positivist view of the judge's decision in a hard case as an act of legislation. These arguments are rejected as out of place by other "positivists", who emphasize that the answer must come from the legal texts alone (Grodzinsky). Some of our scholars derive their answers to hard cases by the method, described by Dworkin, of resorting to general legal principles and interpretive theories of the law as a whole (Kook, Herzog). We have also seen how *posqim* will attribute legal argumentation to support the rulings of those with whom they disagree (Feinstein, Herzog). In so doing, they provide evidence for the realist conception of judicial reasoning as the formal justification for a decision that is "really" warranted by goals that lie outside the judge's reasons.

As noted above, theories developed for the analysis of secular law are not a perfect fit with a religious system, and within their own jurisprudential sphere these theories are controversial. With these caveats in mind, however, they offer a helpful perspective for grasping the essentially *indeterminate* nature of the *halakhah* on controversial questions such as ours. Our results indicate that *halakhah*, like other legal systems, offers no one "correct" answer to questions disputed by its authorities (or, as a Dworkinian might say, no one "correct" answer on which all those authorities can agree). In itself, of course, this observation is hardly news. *Mahloqet*, halakhic dispute, has been regarded as an inevitable feature of rabbinic law at least since tanaitic times, yet it is a feature that has caused considerable discomfort to many. If some authorities look upon it with equanimity, others are distressed at its implicit threat to the unity of the Torah and the effectiveness of Jewish law.[85] Accordingly, we witness attempts throughout halakhic history to reduce the scope of this legal uncertainty. Criteria for decision-making, *kelalei hapesaq* of divine as well as human origin, appear to help the rabbis blaze the trail of halakhic truth through the wilderness of *mahloqet*. "Codes" are compiled to serve as digests of those interpretations of the law that the codifiers view as correct. Precedent, in the form of the emerging *halakhic* consensus, works to distinguish the correct view of the law from other possible and even plausible interpretations. Eventually, the "right" answer will be identified with the opinion which commands the assent of a preponderance of *halakhists* over a significant period of time, and the minority opinions, though studied avidly in the *yeshivah*, will lose whatever authoritative power they once possessed. The achievement of consensus, it can be argued, is an indispensable aspect of rabbinic legal practice; how else, in the absence of a Sanhedrin that could declare the law by fiat, is one to know what "the" *halakhah* demands on any given issue?[86] And it is perhaps just as indispensable that the system itself view the emergence of consensus opinion as the reflection of the ongoing Divine will. The *gedolei hador*, the recognized *halakhic* decisors, derive the proper judgement through the dispassionate, value-free exercise of logic and analysis upon the relevant sacred texts. In this sense, they can be said to function as "oracles" of the law, its interpreters and not its legislators.[87]

The method employed in this study suggests that these attempts to force an objective correctness upon *halakhic* decision are doomed to failure. If our findings with respect to the responsa on conversion hold true for other areas of Jewish law (and there is no *prima faciae* reason to suppose they do not), then rabbinic discretion is endemic to the *halakhic* process as a whole. In addressing hard cases, that is, rabbis cannot avoid the necessity of making choices. They choose whether to subject their texts to narrow or broad construction; they choose whether to resort to policy considerations (and which considerations those shall be) as a means of resolving legal ambiguity; they choose whether to take judicial notice of opposing viewpoints; they choose which rulings of their predecessors shall serve as precedents; they choose whether to adhere to the established legal standard or to deviate from it. All of these *choices*, which as we have seen lead directly to the *poseq*'s final ruling and which taken together constitute the general perception of the objective *halakhah*, are acts of rabbinic discretion. No preexisting legal norm, no canon of legal logic forces the *poseq* to make one choice over its alternative. It is his will rather than his reason, a will presumably informed by his faith, his adherence to standards of reasonability in interpretation, his sense of the purposes of the law, and his assessment of the needs of the community against the backdrop of Jewish history, that determines his choice. All of which suggests that the process of *halakhic* decision is much more art than it is science.

3. From this point, we may draw a conclusion with special application to liberal *halakhah*. One of the major objections raised against our enterprise, by critics of the left as well as the right, is that liberal *halakhah* is unprincipled. That is, liberal (especially Reform) rabbis who write on *halakhic* subjects lack carefully delineated principles to determine how their decisions ought to be made, to decide which traditional laws to retain and which to abandon. Ultimately, say these critics, Reform responsa writers make their decisions on an *ad hoc* basis, relying exclusively upon considerations of expediency and personal prejudice. Put differently, they reach the same decisions at which they would have arrived in the absence of their *halakhic* argumentation and its marshalling of traditional sources. Reform responsa thus lose any claim to the objective validity and the logical consistency which mark the traditional *halakhic* process.[88] There is much of value in this criticism, even if those who raise it are probably averse to the idea of any Reform "*halakhic* process", principled or otherwise. Liberal *halakhah*, if it is to be more than an exercise in dredging up sources merely to endorse the preconceived religious sensibilities and biases of liberal Jews, must be prepared to justify its conclusions by means of principles more permanent and general than the need to arrive at an "expedient" decision in the case at hand.[89] Consistency and objectivity are surely worthy goals for any humanistic endeavor; they are building blocks of intellectual

integrity. This criticism is nonetheless flawed, quite apart from the problem of imputing objective standards of knowledge to the humanities and to law in general, because it exaggerates the objectivity of traditional rabbinic responsa. As our analysis demonstrates, the *halakhah* in this hard case is indeterminate precisely because the rabbinic respondents do not (and presumably cannot) derive their conclusion without making choices between available alternatives. No calculus exists to fix with any precision how these choices are to be made, to identify which methods of reasoning are to be employed, which precedents are to be held authoritative, which policy considerations are to be brought into play and how much weight is to be attributed to them. And the responsa in which these choices occur are all perfectly "Orthodox"; no one questions their legitimacy as documents of *halakhah*. Our own responsa, afflicted as they are with the same essential indeterminacy, are thus not that different in style from their Orthodox counterparts.

Our own efforts, therefore, cannot be disqualified as non-*halakhic*. Our conclusions, to be sure, will differ from those drawn by Orthodox *halakhists*. For us, there are many more "hard questions" than there are for them, much more indeterminacy, many more choices to make. And Orthodox *posqim* will make different choices than do we, given that their notion of a fit or proper response to a hard question will often diverge radically from ours. None of this, however, should obscure from our view that the fact of choice, of discretion, is a necessary and inevitable element of Jewish normative thinking.[90] As we have seen, the *posqim* utilize a variety of methods to justify their choices. Of particular interest to us might be the argument of the "pragmatists" who argue that the correct answer may well be the one which affords the best consequences, the one which stands as the most effective means to secure an agreed-upon end, even when it deviates from the commonly-held legal rule. One would be hard put to find a better description of the central tendency of liberal *halakhah*. Differences in result, it would seem, do not necessarily mean a difference in nature or essence. This last point, which grows out of a study of *halakhic* responsa through the prism of the literature of contemporary jurisprudence, suggests that the field of legal theory has much to offer us toward the understanding of *halakhah* in general and of liberal *halakhah* in particular.

Notes

* I am indebted to two of my students at HUC-JIR-Cincinnati, whose rabbinical theses helped in no small measure to direct my thinking on the issues covered in this essay. They are Rabbi Ilene Lerner Bogosian (*"Discourage with the Left Hand and Draw Near with the Right": An Exploration of Ambivalence Toward Gerim in Jewish Law and Practice*, 1992) and Rabbi Mark Bryan Goldfarb (*An Analysis of Modern Responsa on the Question of Proper Motivations for Conversion*, 1991). *Harbeh lamadeti mirabbotai...(Ta'anit* 7a).

1. This acceptance, known as *qabalat ha-mitzvot*, is taken quite seriously. While all the steps of the conversion ritual are in theory to take place before a *Bet Din*, if circumcision and/or immersion are performed outside that context they are valid *bedi'avad*. Not so *qabalat hamitzvot*: should that statement be made in the presence of two rather than three judges, or at night, etc., it and the conversion are not considered valid at all. *Shulhan Arukh Yoreh Deah* 268:3 and *Taz*, n. 9, in the name of R. Asher (b. *Yeb.* 4:31).

2. b. *Bekhorot* 30b.

3. See the position of R. Nechemyah and R. Yehudah, Tractate *Gerim* 1:7 (1:3, ed. Higger), cited as well in *Yeb.* 24b. The clear distinction between *gerei 'arayot* (i.e., the Samaritans, who converted out of fear of wild beasts; *cf.* II Kings 17:24-41) and "true proselytes" is maintained by the *setam Talmud* in b. *Baba Kama* 38b, b. *Sanhedrin* 85b, b. *Hullin* 3b, and b. *Niddah* 56b. And see below for the discussion of the opinions of Rabbis Kook and Herzog on this question.

4. M. *Ye.* 2:8: one who is suspected of a sexual liaison with a Gentile woman who has since converted may not marry her; if, however, he does marry her, she remains his legitimate wife. The *Talmud* (24b) draws the conclusion that her conversion is valid (*hagiyoret miha havya*) and cites the statement of Rav that those who convert out of ulterior motives are valid proselytes. This, I should stress, is the predominant view of the "final" *halakhah*; as we shall see, some contemporary *posqim* question whether modern-day insincere conversions qualify as valid.

5. See the version of Rav's ruling preserved in *Y. Kid.* 4:1. The *rishonim* suggest another justification. Even though the original conversion may have been prompted out of ulterior motivations, once the proselyte has begun to observe the commandments we can presume that he or she has subsequently accepted the obligation to do so (*agav onsaiho gamru veqiblu*), in much the same way as a person who is coerced into selling his property can be said to have consented to the sale, after the fact, as a result of the pressure brought to bear upon him (*b. Baba Batra* 47b-48a). See Ritva and *Nimukei Yosef* to *Yeb.* 24b. Here we find the roots of a distinction, of great importance to *poskim* such as Kook and Herzog, between "insincere" converts who observe the *mitzvot* and "insincere" converts who do not.

6. *b. Yeb.* 24b, *Tosafot, s.v. lo, Yad, Hil. Issurei Bi'ah* 13:15.

7. *Yad, Is. Bi'ah* 13:14-18 and 14:1 (but see below, in the discussion of Rav Kook's decision, for another interpretation of Rambam's ruling); *Shulhan Arukh Yoreh Deah* 268:12 and *Bi'ur Hagra ad loc.*

8. Legal textbooks are indeed likely to be cited as "authorities" in judicial decisions, as all who are familiar with names such as Blackstone, Wigmore, and Prosser can testify. The point is that these authorities are not legislators. Like Rambam and the *Shulhan Arukh*, they describe the law, but they do not make it. For a full treatment of the distinction between codification in Jewish law and in other systems see Menachem Elon, *Hamishpat Ha'ivri* (Jerusalem, 1988), pp. 938-948.

9. *b. Shabbat* 31a, *b. Menachot* 44a; *Tosafot, b. Yeb.* 24b, *s.v. lo.*

10. *Beit Yosef, Yoreh Deah* 268, fol. 215b; *Siftei Kohen, Shulhan Arukh Yoreh Deah* 268, no. 23.

11. The "classic" treatment of this theme (*i.e.*, one which delineates the issues which subsequent scholars return to and address) is Benjamin Cardozo, *The Nature of the Judicial Process*, New Haven, 1921.

12. Cardozo's "method of philosophy"; *ibid.*, ch. 1.

13. Such as the "rule of recognition" proposed by H.L.A. Hart, *The Concept of Law* Oxford, 1961, the most influential of the contemporary legal positivists. Hart's work is a sympathetic critique of John Austin, *The Province of Jurisprudence Determined* (London, 1832), whose theory of "law as the command of the sovereign" developed a line of thought laid down by Hobbes and Bentham which was critical of natural law philosophy. Law, for positivists, is a strictly human enactment, whose source is to be found not in reason or nature but in social and political choices made within the context of a particular legal system. A similar "master rule" is Hans Kelsen's *grundnorm*; see *The Pure Theory of Law*, tr. Max Knight, Berkeley and Los Angeles, 1967.

14. After the famous aphorism of Justice Holmes in his dissent in *Southern Pacific Co. v. Jensen*, 244 U.S. 205, 221 (1917). Cardozo, p. 113, concurs that unlike a proper legislature the judge "legislates only between the gaps", within the "open spaces" of the law.

15. Ronald Dworkin, *Taking Rights Seriously*, Cambridge, MA, 1977, and *Law's Empire* Cambridge, MA, 1986.

16. This determination of the law by non-enacted principles resembles natural law theory, but as Bernard Jackson notes, it differs in one important respect. Dworkin's "right answer" is derived from the morality and political values of a particular community and not from universal reason or morality. See Jackson, *Semiotics and Legal Theory*, London, 1985, p. 7.

17. See especially Jerome N. Frank, *Law and the Modern Mind*, New York, 1930. The central themes of legal realism have been taken up and developed by the Critical Legal Studies movement, which sees the development of law as determined by the political worldview of societies and legal elites. See Mark Kelman, *A Guide to Critical Legal Studies*, Cambridge, MA, 1987. Some of the strongest criticism of legal realism as an explanation of how judges make decisions comes from judges themselves. See Aharon Barak, *Judicial Discretion*, New Haven, 1989, pp. 37-38, who questions whether even the extremists among these groups truly believe that judicial discretion exists in every case.

18. See John Dewey, "Logical Method and Law", 10 *Cornell Law Quarterly* (1924), 17ff. Such institutional requirements, rather than any inherent logic in the law and its rules, account for the tremendous consistency and stability in judicial decision within a particular system; Karl Llewellyn, *The Common Law Tradition* (Chicago, 1960).

19. The point is stressed by Shalom Albeck, *Mishpat Umusar Bemesoret Yisrael, Mehkarei Mishpat*, v 1, 1980, pp 40-57.

20. See Avraham Z. Rabinovits, *He'arot Lanoseh Mediniut Hilkhatit Vehandasah Genetit, Techumin*, v. 2, 1981, pp. 504-512.

21. Thus, for example, Menachem Elon adopts the *Grundnorm* of Kelsen and the legal sources described in Salmond's *Jurisprudence* as descriptive of the Jewish legal system. In this, he is followed closely by Joel Roth, *The Halakhic Process: A Systemic Analysis* (New York, 1986, and see the review essay by Gordon Tucker in *Judaism*, v. 38, Summer, 1989, pp. 365-376). See also Norman Lamm and Aaron Kirschenbaum, "Freedom and Constraint in the Jewish Juridical Process", 1 *Cardozo Law Review* (1979), 99-133; Elliot N. Dorff, "A Methodology for Jewish Medical Ethics", B.S. Jackson and S.M. Passamaneck, eds., *Jewish Law Association Studies VI*, especially at pp. 46 ff.; and Bernard S. Jackson, "Secular Jurisprudence and the Philosophy of Jewish Law", *Jewish Law Annual*, Boston, 1987, v. 6, pp. 3-44, as well as the other articles in that volume.

22. H. Ben-Menahem, *Judicial Deviation in Talmudic Law*, Chur, Switzerland, 1991.

23. On legal pragmatism and its relationship to the realist school, see Richard Posner's introduction to his *The Problems of Jurisprudence*, Cambridge, MA, 1990.

24. Take our case as an illustration. Hillel and R. Hiyya (note 9, above) accepted proselytes who came to us for motives other than *leshem shamayim*. The stories in which those cases are reported do not offer any legal justification for their decisions, which allows us to speculate that these authorities may hold that no justification is necessary, *i.e.*, the rabbi enjoys unfettered discretion in the law of conversion. The *Tosafists* and the later commentators, however, explain these actions on the ground that the rabbis were certain that the converts would eventually practice Judaism out of sincere religious motivations. In thus justifying the cases, later *halakhah* suggests a limit upon rabbinic discretion which is not enunciated explicitly in the original sources.

25. Mark Washofsky, "The Search for Liberal *Halakhah*", in Walter Jacob and Moshe Zemer, eds., *Dynamic Jewish Law*, Tel Aviv and Pittsburgh, 1991, pp. 25-51, and Walter S. Wurzburger, "The Conservative View of *Halakhah* is Non-Traditional", *Judaism*, v. 58, Summer, 1989, p. 378.

26. See, for example, Shlomo Riskin, *Women and Jewish Divorce*, Hoboken, 1989. Riskin contends that a husband may be coerced into divorcing his wife if she refuses to live with him on the grounds that "he is repulsive to me". He thus exhumes a legal argument that the *halakhic* authorities have overwhelmingly rejected for the last eight hundred years.

27. See David Ellenson, *Tradition in Transition*, Lanham, MD, 1989, pp. 61-100; the articles by J. David Bleich, Marc D. Angel and Shlomo Riskin in Emanuel Feldman and Joel B. Wolowelsky, *The Conversion Crisis*, New York, 1990; S.T. Rubenstein, *Giyur leshem ishut-bahalakhah*, Torah shebe'al peh, v. 13, 1971, pp. 74-81.

28. *Resp. Pe'er Hador*, n. 132. On the authoritative brevity with which Maimonides answers *halakhic* queries see Elon, p. 1233 and n. 78.

29. *M. Yebamot* 2:8 (24b); *Yad, Gerushin* 10:14.

30. The *Talmudic* discussion at *Yebamot* 24b presumes that the maidservant or Gentile woman referred to in the *Mishnah* had no motive other than marriage in converting (or being converted) to Judaism.

31. *Avodah Zarah* 36b; *Yad, Isurei Bi'ah* 12:1-2.

32. *M. Gitin* 5:5; *b. Gitin* 55a. See Rashi on *Gitin* 55a (*s.v. mipney*): if we enforce the Toraitic standard and require the thief to tear down the house in order to retrieve the stolen beam and return it to its rightful owner, he will likely refuse to do so. In other words, we effectively prevent him from doing *teshuvah*. It is better to leave the building standing and allow him to compensate the beam's owner.

33. Rambam's analogy to the *taqanat hasahvim* is, at best, problematic. There, the thief must at least restore the value of the stolen object, if not the object itself; here, the marriage and conversion allow the sinner to keep the fruits of his transgression. This would violate the *Talmudic* principle that the sinner not be permitted to benefit from his action (*b. Yeb.* 92b and parallels cited in *Masoret Hashas*).

34. Compare the *taqanah* of R. Yehudah Hanasi that, in order to encourage thieves to repent, we do not accept payments of compensation from them (*b. Baba Kama* 94b). *Tosafot* (*s.v. bimey*) notes that this contradicts common *Talmudic* practice, where thieves were in fact expected to restore the value of stolen goods. Moreover, were this rule to be taken literally, any thief could pretend to do repentance and thereby exempt himself from the compensation requirement. See *Yad, Gezeilah* 1:13, and *Shulhan Arukh, HM* 366:1.

35. See R. Barukh Halevy Epstein, *Torah Temimah* to Deut. 21:11, n. 72, and below for R. Haim Ozer Grodzinsky's critique of the notion that the *bet din* may violate a "little" commandment to save another from transgressing a "big" one.

36. *Resp. Rashba*, I, no. 1205. I say "virtually" because this case is complicated by the fact that the man who cohabits with the Gentile maidservant is already married. Rashba is incensed at the man's abandonment of wife and child, and this might account in part for his stringent ruling. Nonetheless, Rashba makes clear that the conversion and marriage of the maidservant is a separate wrong, quite apart from the man's betrayal of his first wife.

37. *Yad, Mamrim* 2:4 and commentaries; Elon, pp. 425-426.

38. The best comprehensive treatment of these principles is Eliezer Berkovits, *Hahalakhah: Kocha Vetafkidah* (Jerusalem, 1981). See also Shalom Albeck (note 19, above); Louis Jacobs, *A Tree of Life*, London, 1984, pp. 182-192; Shimeon Federbusch, *Hamusar vehamishpat beyisrael*, Jerusalem, 1947; Boaz Cohen, *Law and Tradition in Judaism*, New York, 1969, pp. 182-238; David Novak, *Halakhah in a Theological Dimension*, Chico, CA, 1985, pp. 11-28; Moshe Silberg, *Kach Darko Shel Talmud* (Jerusalem, 1964), pp. 66-138.

39. P. V. Baker and P. St. J. Langan, *Snell's Principles of Equity*, 28th ed. (London, 1982), pp. 5-22; W. W. Buckland, *Equity in Roman Law* (London, 1911).

40. See Moshe Zemer, "Authority and Criteria in Liberal *Halakhah*," in Walter Jacob and Moshe Zemer, eds., *Dynamic Jewish Law: Progressive Halakhah, Essence and Application* Tel Aviv and Pittsburgh, 1991, pp. 9-24.

41. It is instructive that Berkovits, in his discussion of the principles discussed above, relies almost exclusively upon *Talmudic* sources. The absence of material from codes or responsa leads one to the conclusion that, following the end of its formative period, *halakhah* became much more rule-oriented and less likely to deviate from accepted precedent and *pesaq*. There are, however, some notable exceptions. R. Moshe Isserles violated a rabbinic prohibition and conducted a wedding on the night of *Shabbat* in order to preserve the match and safeguard family reputations (*Resp. Harema*, no. 125). R. Asher b. Yechiel declares that a divorce coerced from a husband when a wife claims that he is repulsive to her is invalid and her offspring by a subsequent husband are *mamzerim*. Yet he departs from his own logic and limits this ruling to future cases only (*Resp. Harosh* 43:6).

42. The formalization of law as a stabilizing and stultifying factor in legal change and judicial flexibility is a theme treated by Sir Henry Maine, *Ancient Law*, London, 1861, pp. 1-59. See also Alan Watson, *The Evolution of Law*, Baltimore, 1985, especially pp. 115-119. Eliezer Berkovits, *Not in Heaven: The Nature and Function of Halakhah*, New York, 1983, pp. 85-112, argues that the codification of Jewish law has robbed the Oral Torah of its original creative energy. S. Z. Havlin suggests that the tendency for later generations to submit to the *halakhic* authority of their predecessors is a literary phenomenon, brought about by the redaction or composition of comprehensive legal works which demand the attention and assent of the community; "*Al 'hachatimah hasifrutit*'," in *Mechkarim Basifrut Hatalmudit*, Lieberman Tribute Volume; Jerusalem, 1983, pp. 148-192.

43. *Resp. Tuv ta'am veda'at*, no. 230. It is unclear whether by "new religion" is meant religious reform or cultural enlightenment and emancipation. To Kluger, at any rate, these phenomena were probably the same thing.

44. Note that Kluger deftly changes the terminology from that submitted to him by his correspondent (assuming that Kluger accurately reproduces the latter's communication). Where in the description of the case we are told that the couple have cohabited several times (*kamah pa'amim*), here we discover that they have been together many times (*harbeh pa'amim*). The strengthened terminology also strengthens Kluger's argument that the man's lust has been quenched so that the request for conversion is not based upon his desire to marry her. On the tendency of judges to restate the facts of a case in order to stack the deck in favor of their decision, see Richard Posner, *Cardozo: A Study in Reputation*, Chicago, 1990, pp. 33-57.

45. On all of this, see *b. Yeb.* 24b and Rashi, *s.v. de'amar rav asi*; *Tosefta Yeb.* 4:5; *Nimukei Yosef* to Alfasi, *Yevamot*, fol. 5b.

46. Isserles, *EHE* 177:5. This raises the issue of precedent in *halakhah*: on what basis does Kluger determine that Isserles' decision concerning an unmarried woman applies to the case of a Gentile spouse? This issue will be discussed below, as part of my analysis of Ouziel's decision.

47. This is Rambam's understanding of R. Yose's statement (*M. Avot* 2:12), "let all your actions be for the sake of Heaven". According to Rambam, this constitutes a demand that the individual harness his entire being and all his actions toward the apprehension of God (Commentary to *Avot*, ch. 5).

48. A rather obvious point: how can we expect of the Gentile spouse-to-be a higher degree of religiosity than that of her intended? Yet the obvious needs at times to be stated. See the discussion of R. Moshe Feinstein, below.

49. *Resp. Imrei Yosher*, v. 1, no. 176. Arik (d. 1925) was one of the leading Galician *halakhic* authorities.

50. *Yad, Isurey Bi'ah* 14:1; *Shulhan Arukh, Yoreh Deah* 268:12.

51. *Resp. Melamed Leho'il*, v. 2, nos. 83 and 85.

52. Consequentialist arguments such as these, strewn throughout Hoffmann's responsa, support the widely-held perception of him as an Orthodox "reformer" of the *halakhah* who issued lenient rulings in a conscious effort to adapt Jewish observance to the challenges of a modern, liberal-secular environment. See Jonathan Brown, *Modern Challenges to Halakhah* (Chicago, 1969).

53. I refer to the statement "the innocent should not suffer for the sins of the guilty" as "extralegal" since it is hardly a universal principle of Jewish law; witness the *agunah* and the *mamzer*. And one searches almost in vain for the contemporary Orthodox halakhist who would agree with Hoffmann's policy judgement that it is better to convert these people ourselves rather than let them go to Reform rabbis.

54. *Resp. Achiezer*, v. 3, no. 26.

55. Lev. 18:19, 29; *Yad, Issurei Bi'ah* 1:1. Grodzinsky assumes, plausibly, that *niddah* is one of the commandments which the currently intermarried couple will violate upon the woman's conversion.

56. *Resp. Da'at Kohen*, nos. 154-155.

57. *Resp. Heikhal Yitzhaq, Even Ha'ezer* 1:1, nos. 19, 20, and 21; *Pesakim Ukhetavim*, Jerusalem, 1990, v. 4, nos. 87, 89, 90, and 91.

58. See above at notes 3, 4, and 5.

59. See Moshe Zemer, "The Rabbinic Ban on Conversion in Argentina", *Judaism*, v. 37, Winter, 1988, pp. 84-96.

60. Kook does provide for the rare "sincere" proselyte: he or she can travel to Jerusalem, to be examined there by Kook's own *bet din*.

61. Dworkin, *Taking Rights Seriously*, pp. 118-123.

62. *Yad, Hil. Issurei Bi'ah* 13:17; *Shulhan Arukh Yoreh Deah* 268:12.

63. Kook relies here upon a distinction used by *Tosafot, Hulin* 3b, *s.v. kasavar*, to explain the *Talmudic* dispute over whether the Samaraitans were valid proselytes. Those who say they are not valid proselytes hold that the Samaritans, who converted originally out of the ulterior motive of fear, never observed Judaism properly. Thus, in Kook's equation, insincerity plus subsequent nonobservance equals an invalid conversion.

64. See note 5, above.

65. This is not to say that such policy considerations cannot lie below the surface of Herzog's rulings. My concern here is with the jurisprudential question of the process by which a rabbinic decision is argued and justified, rather than with the psychological or sociological inquiry as to how a rabbi actually "thinks up" his answers. The former, as the realists would assert, may well be a smokescreen concealing his "real" motivations, but it is through his written argument that a rabbi or a judge influences the future development of the law. On the distinction between these two levels of judicial thinking, see Richard Wasserstrom, *The Judicial Decision*, Stanford, 1961.

66. See *M. Eduyot* 1:5, Rambam *ad loc.* in the Kafich edition of his *Commentary to the Mishnah* and Kafich's note 31.

67. *Resp. Igerot Moshe, Even Ha'ezer*, v. 2, no. 27, and *Yore Deah*, v. 1, no. 160.

68. Although Orthodox halakhists accept Feinstein's judgement concerning Conservative rabbis (J. David Bleich, *Contemporary Halakhic Problems, Volume III* New York, 1989, p. 91 at n. 6), it is subject to the logical -- and jurisprudential -- criticism that the *poseq* assumes facts not in evidence. See Roth, pp. 71-74.

69. See *b. Yevamot* 47a-b (the proselyte is informed of "some [*i.e.*, and not *all*] of the lighter and weightier commandments") and *b. Shabbat* 68a-b (one who converts among the Gentiles is a valid convert, even though out of his ignorance he violates the most important commandments).

70. Compare Feinstein to Kluger, who arrives at his permissive ruling through a similarly forced argument. Unlike Feinstein, Kluger seems to accept that argument as persuasive, so that it is not so obvious that in his case the legal justification is but a "mask" or a "smokescreen" concealing the true motivations of his decision.

71. Feinstein uses the term *me'akev* (an absolute, *sine qua non* requirement) to describe acceptance of the *mitzvot*: without that acceptance, there is no conversion, even *bedi'avad*.

72. Resp. *Mishpetei Uziel*, v. 1, *Yore Deah*, no. 14.

73. See notes 9 and 10, above.

74. The language of *Tosafot, Yeb.* 24b, s.v. *lo*.

75. *Mishpetei Uziel, Even Ha'ezer*, no. 18. He adds that "we are allowed to make ourselves *hedyotot* and facilitate the conversion" in order to combat intermarriage. *Hedyotot* refers to the ignorant judges who improperly converted insincere proselytes during the days of David and Solomon; *Yad, Isurei Bi'ah* 13:15. It is, to say the least, unusual for a *poseq* to look upon these judges as models worthy of our imitation.

76. See *Mishpetei Uziel, EHE*, no. 18: in our day, to combat the threat of intermarriage, it is necessary to convert the Gentile spouse, "relying in this matter upon our teacher, the Rambam".

77. Uziel's language here is not as precise as it might be. The prohibition against this man marrying this woman is certainly *derabanan* (M. *Yeb.* 2:8); the suggestion that to accept an insincere proselyte violates only a rabbinic provision assumes that, *bedi'avad*, the conversion is valid. Elsewhere (*EHE*, no. 18), Uziel states that this is his view. Were he to hold with the authorities who invalidate such conversions, the prohibition would be absolute indeed.

78. On the limits of precedent in Jewish law see Elon, pp. 768-804, and Zorach Warhaftig, "*Hatakdim Bamishpat Ha'ivri*", *Shenaton Hamishpat Ha'ivri*, vols. 6-7 (1979-1980), pp. 105-132.

79. The authors of the *Shulhan Arukh*, for example: R. Yosef Karo declares that the law shall follow the majority view among a panel of leading *rishonim*, while R. Moshe Isserles holds to the rule that "the law is according to the latest authorities". See their introductions to, respectively, the *Bet Yosef* and the *Darkhei Moshe* commentaries to the *Tur*.

80. On the other hand, in *Mishpetei Uziel*, YD, no. 25, he offers an argument of principle. The case of the *yefat to'ar* proves that "whenever the Torah estimates that a man cannot release himself from the grip of the evil impulse, it gives him an opening for repentance so that he might not sin." As we have seen, however, the notion that we are permitted to deviate from *halakhic* standards in the name of some "higher purpose" is *not* a consistent *halakhic* principle. Rambam's reasoning-"better that they eat the sauce than the fat" - and his analogies to *yefat to'ar* and *taqanat hashavim* are contestable, and Rashba is but one example of the countless *posqim* who reject those analogies, explicitly or implicitly. See above at notes 33-35.

81. See note 80 and the discussion of Grodzinsky's responsum, above.

82. Posner, *Problems of Jurisprudence*, p. 95.

83. For an overview see Peter Haas, "The Modern Study of the Responsa," in D. Blumenthal, ed., *Approaches to Judaism in Medieval Times*, v. 2, Chico, CA, 1985, pp. 35-71. The basic monograph is still Solomon B. Freehof, *The Responsa Literature*, Philadelphia, 1955.

84. This is especially true of the *Mishpat Ivri* school, whose leading current representative is Menachem Elon. See his *Hamishpat Ha'ivri*, pp. 1213-1281, and his introductions to the volumes of the *Mafte'ach Hasheelot Vehateshuvot* Jerusalem, 1981--, an index oft the responsa literature of Spain and North Africa during the period of the *rishonim* (ca. 1000- ca. 1500).

85. For example, R. Ya'akov b. Asher in his introduction to *Tur Hoshen Mishpat* complains that every litigant can rely upon that *poseq* who agrees with his position, a practice which runs counter to the search for legal truth. R. Yosef Karo, in his introduction to the *Bet Yosef*, recites a familiar refrain that "the Torah has not become two Torahs; it has become innumerable Torahs, owing to the many books written ostensibly to clarify its laws." On this topic generally, see Menachem Elon, *Meni'im Ve'ekronot Bekodifikatsiah Shel Hahalakhah*, in Y. Eisner, ed., *Hagut vehalakhah*, Jerusalem, 1973, pp. 75-119.

86. See Washofsky, "The Search for a Liberal *Halakhah*". That consensus is a necessary factor in attaining even a modicum of objectivity in law is a point stressed heavily by Posner, *Problems of Jurisprudence*, pp. 125-129.

87. For a succinct statement of this theory, see J. David Bleich, *Contemporary Halakhic Problems I*, New York, 1977, pp. xii-xviii.

88. See Dan Cohn-Sherbok, "Law and Freedom in Reform Judaism", *Journal of Reform Judaism*, v. 30, Winter, 1983, pp. 88-97, and "Law in Reform Judaism: A Study of Solomon Freehof," *Jewish Law Annual*, v. 7, 1988, pp. 198-209. For a response see Walter Jacob and Mark Staitman in the afore-cited *Journal of Reform Judaism*, pp. 98-104. For detailed treatments of Freehof's *halakhic* method, which tend to contradict

Cohn-Sherbok's arguments, see Kenneth Jay Weiss, *Solomon B. Freehof: Reforging the Links*, DHL Dissertation, HUC-JIR (Cincinnati, 1980) and Scott Gurdin, *The Halakhic Methodology of Solomon Freehof*, Rabbinical Thesis, HUC-JIR, Cincinnati, 1991.

89. This criticism bears a striking parallel to that made by Herbert Wechsler of the *ad hoc* fashion in which some American courts during the 1950's decided constitutional questions; "Toward Neutral Principles of Constitutional Law", 73 *Harvard Law Review* 1 (1959).

90. It is sometimes argued that "Jewish normative thinking" includes the discipline of ethics as well as *halakhah* and that *our* normative thinking corresponds more closely with the former than with the latter. This argument rests upon the controversial presumption that there is such a thing as a normative "Jewish" ethics, as opposed to ethics in general. If that presumption is wrong, as I suspect, then those who make this argument have the burden of proving just what precisely is "Jewish" about their approach to normative thinking. See, in general, Menachem Kellner, "Reflections on the Impossibility of Jewish Ethics," *Sefer Bar-Ilan*, vol. 22-23 (1988), pp. 45-52.

RETROACTIVE ANNULMENT OF A CONVERSION
A Survey of Representative *Halakhic* Sources

David Ellenson

The issue of retroactive annulment of a conversion is one that has increasingly commanded the attention of *halakhic* authorities in recent years. In the early 1970's, the government of Israel was almost toppled as a result of this matter. Two children - Hanokh and Miriam - born to Chava and Otto Langer in 1945 and 1947 were declared to be *mamzerim* by the Rabbinical court of Tel Aviv in 1955 when it was discovered that Mrs. Langer had previously been married to an Avraham Borokovsky, who was said to have converted to Judaism in Warsaw.[1] As the Borokovskys separated without obtaining a *get*, Mrs. Borokovsky had no right, according to Jewish law, to remarry. As a result of her failure to disclose this information to the officiating rabbi at the time of her marriage to Otto Langer, the rabbi performed the ceremony.[2] The children born of her subsequent union were therefore illegitimate and, consequently, forbidden by the law from marrying other "kosher Jews."

When one of the children, Hanokh, on May 3, 1966, applied for a marriage license, he was refused permission on the grounds of his illegitimacy. After six years of appeals, Rabbi Shlomo Goren, serving as a head of a rabbinic court whose other members remained unidentified, resolved the problem of *mamzerut* for the Langer children by declaring that Mr. Borokovsky's conversion to Judaism was, in fact, "null and void," as a result, among other reasons, of his failure to observe Jewish law faithfully subsequent to his presumed conversion.[3] As Jewish law does not recognize the possibility of legal betrothal between a Jew and a non-Jew, Mrs. Langer's first marriage to Mr. Borokovsky was no longer seen as valid. The impediment to her marriage to Mr. Langer no longer existed and the stigma of *mamzerut*, with its attendant disabilities, was now removed from Miriam and Hanokh. The Langer children could now be married in Israel. As the *Bet Din* of Rabbi Goren stated on November 19, 1972, "We have decided on 13 *Kislev*, 5733, to permit Hanokh and Miriam Langer, the brother and sister, to enter into the congregation of God and [they are eligible] to marry any Jew according to the religion of Moses and Israel."[4]

The decision was hailed by many for the desired result it achieved. After all, as Rabbi Goren himself explained in the introduction to his decision, "[Hanokh and Miriam Langer's] distress touched my heart deeply. I decided to investigate their bitter fate."[5] Indeed, only the most hard-hearted individual would not have empathized with the plight of the Langer children. Nor could anyone in Israel or abroad fail to celebrate their newly-won freedom to marry. Nevertheless, as commentators such as Amnon Rubenstein, the Dean of Tel Aviv University Law School, pointed out in an op-ed piece in *HaAretz* in the week following the decision, Rabbi Goren's ruling brought to public consciousness the possibility that a conversion could be retroactively annulled on the basis of a convert's failure to observe Jewish law fully subsequent to the conversion.

Nor have such cases of retroactive annulment been confined to Israeli rabbis. In recent years the Law Committee of the Rabbinical Assembly had to confront this problem, as a Palestinian Muslim couple feigned a sincere interest in Judaism and actually underwent conversion with a Conservative rabbi in order to obtain rights as Jews in Israel under the Law of Return. After entering Israel as Jews, their true motivations emerged, much to the embarrassment of the rabbi who conducted these conversions to Judaism. The rabbi then asked the Law Committee if these conversions could be nullified. Rabbi Steve Saltzman, then of Greensboro, North Carolina, authored the responsum, "Nullification of a Conversion," for the Law Committee, and held that as their "intentions were dishonest and fraudulent *ab initio*," it was "acceptable to argue [that] there was no conversion." Only in a case as unusual as this, R. Saltzman implied, was such a conclusion warranted. Even then, Rabbi Morris Shapiro dissented, concluding, "how dare we nullify the conversion of two Arabs."[6]

Both these cases are admittedly unusual and more than a bit sensational. More common is another tendency, as we shall see, that has emerged in recent years concerning the matter of retroactive annulment of conversion. A number of Orthodox legal authorities in both Israel and the Diaspora have declared as "null and void" conversions involving non-observant people who enter the community of Israel for the sake of marriage to a Jew. The issue addressed in this paper is neither simply theoretical nor exotic. It analyses and describes a matter that is of genuine concern to the practical life of our people.

Classical Sources and Rulings

The classical source in rabbinic literature describing the laws, procedures, and attitudes governing conversion is found in *Yevamot* 47b. There, in the sentences relevant to our concerns, it states, "If he accepted [the yoke of the commandments], he is circumcised forthwith.'... 'As soon as he is healed, arrangements are made for his immediate ablution'... 'When he comes up after his ablution, he is deemed to be an Israelite in all respects.' In respect of what practical issue? In that if he retracted and then betrothed the daughter of an Israelite, he is regarded as a non-conforming Israelite and his betrothal is valid."

The point that emerges here is that once an individual has converted to Judaism, that individual is deemed a Jew regardless of his or her subsequent conduct. *Tosefta Demai* 2:4, puts it succinctly and clearly. The *Tosefta* states, "A proselyte who accepted all the teachings of Torah, though he is suspected of ignoring one religious law, or even the entire Torah, is considered an apostate."

Professor Saul Lieberman, commenting on the meaning of this statement, observed, "That is to say, even if he transgressed the entire Torah, his [status of] Jewishness is not removed."[7] The *Talmud*, in *Bekhorot* 30b, repeats the statement of the *Tosefta* and asserts, as did *Yevamot*, that even if the proselyte betroths a woman after his relapse into non-Jewish ways, "his betrothal is valid - *v'qidushav qidushin*," and his wife must receive a divorce before she is permitted to remarry.

The notion that a conversion, once performed, is valid and cannot be revoked, is reaffirmed in *Yevamot* 24b. There Rabbi Nehemiah states that when conversions are performed for an ulterior motive, the persons involved "are not proselytes - *Einan gerim*." However, in the name of Rav, the *gemara* quickly contends, "The *halakhah* is in accordance with the opinion of him who maintained that they are all [proper] proselytes."

Particularly noteworthy is that all these positions were embodied in rabbinic decisions and codified by later rabbinic authorities as law. In the Middle Ages, a responsum of Rabbi Yehudai, eighth century Gaon of Sura, tells of a converted slave who returned to "his gentile state." Now he wanted to be a Jew once again. Rabbi Yehudai was asked to rule on this man's current status. Was he a Jew, or was he a gentile-in which case *hatafat dam brit* would have to be drawn from him? Rabbi Yehudai unequivocally ruled that despite his apostasy, the man "does not return to his original uncircumcised state - *eino hozer l'areilato harishonah*." Rather, in accordance with *Talmudic* law, he is "an apostate Jew - *Yisrael m'shumad*." As such, no drop of blood need be drawn from him. His status as a Jew is unchangeable.[8]

Maimonides, in his *Mishneh Torah*, *Hilkhot Issurei Bi'ah* 13:17, indicates that even if an individual reverts to his gentile state, he is akin to an "apostate Jew" and "his betrothal is valid." The *Shulhan Arukh*, *Yoreh Deah* 268:2, issues the same ruling.

Furthermore, in *Yoreh Deah* 268:12, these rulings are further established as normative Jewish law. Caro states, "...[If the proselyte] was circumcised and immersed before three common people, behold he is a convert even if it is known that he converted for an ulterior motive. Since he was circumcised and immersed, he has departed from the gentile community ..., and even if he reverted and served idols, behold he is now an apostate Jew whose betrothal is valid."

On the basis of these sources, retroactive annulment of a conversion would appear to be an impossibility in Jewish law. Conversion to Judaism, regardless of motive or subsequent behavior, appears to be an irreversible status. This view is reinforced by statements found in both the *Mishneh Torah* and the *Shulhan Arukh* concerning the conversion of infants to Judaism. While both codes indicate that an infant who is ritually immersed under the agency of a rabbinic court has the right - when he or she reaches the age of majority - to protest and thereby legally reject their Jewish status, should he or she fail to do so, then in the words of Maimonides, *Hilkhot Mohalim* 10:3, "he forfeits [his right] to do so again - *shuv eino yakol limhot.*" He is "a righteous proselyte." Moreover, commentators upon the *Shulhan Arukh, Yoreh Deah* 268:8, add that even should such a convert later apostatize, "the law is that he is considered an apostate Jew - *Dino k'yisrael mumar,*" not a gentile.

The permanency and immutability of the convert's status as a Jew can be seen in the rulings of leading contemporary respondents. Representative of them are the decisions of Rav Kook, the Chief Rabbi of Palestine during the period of the British Mandate. In one responsum, Rav Kook dealt with the case of a presumed convert who had reverted to his original faith. While there was no actual document attesting to his conversion, R. Kuk basing himself upon Yoreh Deah 268.10 and *Hilkhot Issurei Bi'ah* 13:9, stated that if there was evidence that this man had once conducted himself in the ways of Israel there is the "presumption-*hazaqah*" that he is a Jew. Moreover, even if such a person later apostatized, "the law is that he is like any non-observant Jew, even after the apostasy - *Hahamarah*." Clearly, subsequent conduct, no matter how distasteful from the viewpoint of Judaism, could not annul a conversion.[9]

R. Kook's commitment to this position is evident in another responsum he wrote concerning the irreversibility of conversion. In this case, R. Kook speaks of a woman who married a particularly nasty man who had converted to Judaism. This man converted only in order to marry this Jewish woman. However, he was never observant. Moreover, he mistreated his wife and subsequently, after abandoning her, chose a gentile woman. His mean-spiritedness and lack of sincerity were further reflected in his refusal to issue his Jewish wife a *get*. Her local rabbis wanted to alleviate her pain as an *agunah* by "retroactively annulling the conversion - *al y'dei bitul hagerut l'mafre-a*." However, R. Kook, despite his stated sympathies for the Jewish woman, refused to authorize an annulment of the conversion. While he was most sorry that a convert like this had ever been accepted into Judaism, his status as a Jew could not be undone. The law, in R. Kook's view, was clear.[10]

In light of our survey of the sources, R. Kook's position - however sympathetic one might be to the plight of this abandoned Jewish wife - seems incontrovertible from the standpoint of Jewish law. A conversion, once performed, can seemingly not be annulled, regardless of motive or behavior. The justification for a different stance on this issue, and the reasoning and conditions that support it, are the focus of the next section of this paper.

Grounds and Factors Supporting Annulment

In the early twentieth century, Rabbi Nathan Wiedenfeld of Galicia, on the basis of a statement attributed to Rabbi Meier in *Bekhorot* 30a - "A convert who is suspected of ignoring one religious law is suspected of ignoring the entire Torah," avers that a convert's non-observance of Jewish law after the conversion rituals have been complete constitutes an annulment of the conversion. A sincere affirmation of *qabbalat ol mitzvot*, the acceptance of the yoke of the commandments, is a necessary prerequisite for a valid conversion. The convert's subsequent failure to obey the prescriptions of Jewish law indicates that the convert was probably insincere when he initially pledged loyalty to "the yoke of the commandments." Later non-observance by the convert permits a rabbinic authority, R. Wiedenfeld states, to infer that he intentionally was absent during the act of *qabbalat ol mitzvot*. The act of affirmation, in the case of such a convert, is a deception. This judgment of initial insincerity on the basis of later actions had its source, R. Wiedenfeld claims, in a passage in the Rambam, who writes in *Hilkhot Issurei Bi'ah* 13:16, that when a convert reverts to idol-worship, "his ultimate actions demonstrates his initial insincerity - *hohi-ah sofon al tehilaton*." Consequently, "the conversion," R. Wiedenfield maintains, "is retroactively annulled - *batel hagerut l'mafre-a*." Sincere "acceptance of the yoke of the commandments" as displayed through subsequent observance is a prerequisite, in this view, for a valid conversion. Without it, the convert, regardless of the rites he has undergone, has never become a member of the Jewish people. For the first time in this discussion, the notion of intention is introduced as a consideration of primary importance in determining the legitimacy of the conversion.[11]

Lithuanian Rabbi Chaim Ozer Grodzinski (Ahiezer), 1863-1939, makes the identical point and also maintains that a failure to wholeheartedly accept "the yoke of the commandments" retroactively annuls a conversion. The proselyte, at the moment of conversion, is required to accept "the Torah and commandments ... with a whole heart - *b'lev shalem*." If it is obvious to the rabbinic court that an individual will not fully observe Jewish law, then it is equally clear that the prospective convert's affirmation is a deceitful one. "If this is so," Rabbi Ozer writes, "this assumption indicates that he did not accept the yoke of the commandments with a pure heart." Consequently, the conversion, regardless of the other rites performed by the would-be convert under the supervision of a rabbinic court, is invalid.[12]

R. Abraham Dov Baer Kahane Shapira of Kovno, a colleague of R. Ozer, took note of Ahiezer's ruling and observed that in the twentieth century nearly all persons who convert do so for purposes of intermarriage. It is apparent, Kahane maintained, that virtually none of these persons, regardless of the promises they make to a rabbinic court, will become observant Jews. R. Kahane was sensitive to the thrust of the *Talmudic* sources and codes cited in the first part of this paper. Should the individual have undergone circumcision and immersion, and pledged to observe the commandments before a rabbinic court, it would seem, according to the *halakhah*, that the person would now be a Jew whose conversion could not be retroactively annulled. R. Kahane based this latter assumption on the commentaries of the Ritba and Nimuqei Yosef on *Yevamot* 24b. These authorities asserted that even if the proselyte's pledge of fidelity to the commandments was insincere, the social reality of the pre-modern Jewish community was such that the assumption could be made that the individual would be an observant Jew despite his own proclivities and tastes. The content of his promise would be fulfilled despite his lack of intention and this, these *rishonim* ruled, was sufficient to affirm the validity of the conversion.

Rabbi Kahane made due note of this ruling and noted that Jewish law held that these persons, once they had converted, permanently enjoyed the status of Jews. However, he continued, "I fear that this [law] is not applicable in our day." In an earlier period, the social situation of the Jews was such that if a proselyte "did not conduct himself as a Jew and punctiliously observe the commandments," a Jewish woman would not live with him "nor would the Jewish community absorb him." In our day, such is not the case. Most Jews are non-observant and no conditions exist that allow one to assume that such a convert will be observant. The category of societal "coercion" that allowed the Ritba and Nimukei Yosef to adopt their position no longer obtains in the contemporary period.[13]

R. Kahane's reasoning here is fascinating and it reflects the impact that social *realia* often have upon the content and practice of Jewish law. As R. Joel Roth, Dean of the Rabbinical School at the Jewish Theological Seminary has observed, there are many instances in the history of *halakhah* where an "original sociological reality" provides an "underlying assumption" for a particular *halakhic* norm. "The norm," writes R. Roth, "continued to be justifiable" so long as the reality remained unchanged. However, "when a changed social reality vitiated this assumption, the new sociological reality permitted the historical sources of the original norm to become legally relevant and to influence the determination of the law."[14]

Roth's observation illuminates R. Kahane's ruling in this instance. Kahane, it should be emphasized, has contended that proper intention was crucial, in the eyes of every legal authority, to the legality of the conversion process. *It was only the reality of social and religious conditions under which the Jewish people previously lived that permitted earlier generations of rabbis to overlook the purity of a convert's motive and to assert with confidence that a convert would fulfill the conditions of his promise to observe the commandments regardless of his intentions.* While this was not ideal, it was sufficient for the rabbis to rule that a conversion could not be retroactively annulled. As such conditions no longer exist in the world of twentieth century Jewry, the force of the Ritba's ruling no longer is in effect.

Several other authorities take the same position and offer the same rationale for it as R. Kahane. Representative of them are Rabbis Yaakov Breisch (1895-1976) of Switzerland, Isaac Halevi Herzog (1888-1859) of Israel, and Moshe Feinstein (1895-1986) of the United States. In one responsum, R. Breisch contended that the Jewish partners in most cases of intermarriage were themselves "sinners - *poshim.*" As a result, R. Breisch maintained that it was a virtual certainty that their non-Jewish spouses, even when they affirmed an acceptance of the commandments, would be non-observant. Basing himself upon passages in both the *Shulhan Arukh, Yoreh Deah* 268, and Maimonides, *Hilkhot Issurei Biah* 13, R. Breisch held that a failure to accept the yoke of the commandments in sincerity annuls a conversion. In instances such as these, where a would-be proselyte intends to marry a non-observant Jew, what possibility is there that such a person's affirmation is genuine? "We know with certainty," R. Breisch writes, "that their intention is not to convert completely," for their prospective marriage partner, "the Jew scoffs at all [the law] and is only a secular-national Jew. ...[Thus], even if we believe her and acknowledge that her intention is to be a Jew, her intention is essentially to be a 'secular-national' one, without [observance] of the Sabbath, *niddah*, or other commandments, like her husband. A conversion such as this, even a *posteriori*, is not legal." Only an observable fulfillment of the commandments subsequent to conversion can clarify the convert's true intent and establish her identity and status as a legitimate Jew, "a righteous proselyte." Quoting Maimonides and several other talmudic sources and rabbinic authorities, R. Breisch states that only when we see that their righteousness is evident, do we affirm the validity of a conversion. Failure to accept the commandments as evidenced through non-fulfillment of the *mitzvot* "annuls a conversion even a *postfactum.*" The conditions of the modern world indicate that most so-called proselytes fall into this category. Their conversions, even when conducted by an Orthodox *Bet Din* with circumcision and immersion, are invalid.[15]

R. Herzog, in one responsum, dealt with the issue of a gentile woman who desired to convert and was already married civilly to a Jew. R. Herzog was asked whether it was permissible to convert this woman to Judaism. He began by noting that Maimonides, in the twelfth century, had permitted this on the grounds that "it is better that one should taste the skim of the forbidden than its essence." In other words, such conversions do not represent a *halakhic* ideal. However, the Rambam, in effect, was stating that there was room for leniency here and, as a matter of social policy for the community, it was probably wise to adopt the lenient precedent and allow it to guide the ruling in this instance. R. Herzog took due note of this citation. Nevertheless, he dismissed it as inapplicable in the contemporary setting. In the past, Jews were not sinners. "But in our days, to our great sorrow, ... many sinners among the people Israel are leaders of the community even leaders of the nation ..." What does it mean, in such an era as ours, for a gentile to pledge that he or she accepts the commandments of Judaism? Why should they observe the *mitzvot*," R. Herzog queried, "when so many Jews do not observe?" The validity of their pledge to accept the commandments must perforce be in doubt, "as the reason for their conversion is, [in most instances], externally [motivated]." While R. Herzog, in this case, dealt with the issue of conversion *ab initio*, not *post factum*, the direction of his thought parallels that of R. Breisch and others cited in this section. The sociological conditions of the present age lead him to a particular application and understanding of Jewish law as the one he deems appropriate in the contemporary setting.[16]

In another instance, R. Herzog ruled directly on the issue under consideration in this paper - retroactive annulment of a conversion. He cites the Ritba on *Yevamot* 24b, and notes that even when a convert was insincere in acceptance of the yoke of the commandments, the conversion was still considered valid. This was because "in those days a Jew who did not observe the Torah would suffer much [shame in the sight] of his brothers. ... In our days," stated R. Herzog, echoing a theme present in his other writing, "it is possible to transgress all parts of the Torah dealing with the commandments between persons and God, and [still] be a leader, a great prince of Israel ..." The notion of "coercion" that emerged from the social conditions of a bygone era and which permitted the Ritba and the Nimuqei Yosef to assert that the would-be proselyte's conversion was valid, even though his intention was deceitful and insincere, no longer applied. Even the Ritba would assert, in light of the state of contemporary Jewry, "that all conversions in our day fall into a category of doubt."[17] The social reality of modern day western Jewry, where freedom and license have led to a disturbing diminution in traditional Jewish commitment and practice, has made the category of "coercion" inoperable at the present. The failure of converts to fulfill the conditions of their promise to observe the commandments demands that these so-called conversions be annulled retroactively in the modern world.

R. Moshe Feinstein, in his *Iggerot Moshe*, dealt with this issue in several responsa. One will suffice to illustrate his position.[18] In this case, R. Feinstein speaks to the general state of conversion in the United States. Aware that most conversions in the United States are conducted under non-Orthodox auspices, R. Feinstein notes that conversions performed by a Conservative rabbinic court are, by definition, invalid. The rabbis who sit on such a court do not even qualify as "common people," who, as we have seen, are permitted to constitute a valid rabbinic court for purposes of conversion. All Conservative conversions are "null and void." There is no issue of "retroactive annulment" involved here.

R. Feinstein continues by asserting that even if a conversion is conducted by an Orthodox rabbinical court, where one can legitimately assume that circumcision (or *hatafat dam brit*) and immersion were properly carried out, subsequent non-observance of the commandments annuls the conversion. "The essence of conversion," R. Feinstein maintained, is sincere acceptance of the yoke of the commandments. In the case of converts who later disobey Jewish law, "it is obvious, even though he orally affirmed his acceptance of the commandments, that he possessed mental reservations." While one might contend that the would-be convert's intent at the moment of acceptance would be sufficient to establish true intent, Rabbi Feinstein rejected this as unacceptable. For such a person to be presumed a Jew, he would have to perform the commandments. Yet, in this case, he never did so. His promises and affirmations before the rabbinic court were simply "empty talk designed to deceive the rabbinic court. Since he did not [sincerely] accept the commandment, he is not a proselyte and his betrothal is nothing."

These responsa reflect the dramatic impact the modern world has had upon the application of the *halakhah* in this area for many *halakhic* authorities. Yet, as in many other areas of the *halakhah*, there is hardly unanimous agreement among rabbinic authorities as to the appropriateness of this application. The paper will conclude by noting two prominent dissenters from this trend- Rabbi Isser Yehuda Unterman, Rabbi Herzog's successor as Chief Ashkenazic Rabbi of Israel, and Rabbi Ben-Zion Meir Uziel (1880-1953), the first Chief Sephardic Rabbi of the Jewish State.

Final Considerations

Rabbi Unterman, in an article on the laws of conversion and their application, dealt specifically with the question of a potential convert who the rabbinic court knows is most unlikely to observe the commandments. Like the rabbis mentioned in the previous section, there is a context for his confronting the issue. In Rabbi Unterman's case, it is the arrival on Israeli shores of a vast body of intermarried Russian immigrants who are unfamiliar with Judaism and its practices. The question was not merely a theoretical one. It was of great urgency for him and the community and State of Israel.

Returning to the sources cited at the outset of this paper, Rabbi Unterman, like R. Kook, contended that a proper acceptance of the commandments is effectuated when the convert, at the moment of conversion, "accepts upon himself with no mental reservations, the observance of the commandments." Employing Maimonides as a warrant, R. Unterman states, "If a convert later transgresses the commandments, this does not legally impair his conversion." A convert, immediately after his immersion, is a Jew and if he subsequently violates Jewish law, he is simply a "sinful Jew." Like Rav Kook, R. Unterman ruled that the betrothal of such a Jew is valid, "for after immersion, he is a Jew in every respect." In other words, retroactive annulment of a conversion conducted properly before a qualified rabbinic court is unthinkable. If one, *a posteriori*, "has already converted, it is impossible to annul it."

Furthermore, R. Unterman believed that it was undesirable to do so. In this age, even where it is as unlikely as the miracle of "the splitting of the Red Sea" that most converts will be observant, "we are certainly obliged to take pity on the integrity of the family and look at its predicament from the viewpoint of our holy Torah ..." the rabbinate should do nothing to distance Jews from participation in the Jewish community, particularly when the *halakhah* contains lenient precedents that allow the entry of such persons into the Jewish people. Certainly, retroactive annulment of conversion would be an unwise policy for the community to adopt in our age.[19]

R. Uziel, in his responsa, addressed the matter of retroactive annulment of conversion directly. Relying upon the sources referred to at the beginning of this paper, he stated succinctly, "Even if they were not proselytized before a proper rabbinic court, they are proselytes fit for marriage. Their marriage is valid even if they reverted [to their non-Jewish faith]. There is no authority to annul their conversion and marriage and to turn them into non-Jews, not them, and even less, their children."[20] R. Uziel's, as well as R. Unterman's, position on this matter was certainly informed by his view that "we do not," as he wrote elsewhere, "want to lock the door before proselytes." [21] Indeed, it is a commandment, he stated, "to bring them near and to enter them into the covenant of the Torah of Israel."[22]

Conclusion

As Rabbi Moshe Zemer has pointed out in his article, "Authority and Criteria of Liberal *Halakhah*," there are several principles that characterize a liberal approach to *Halakhah*. Among them are the notions that the *Halakhah* is pluralistic, that the ethical is the essence of the *Halakhah*, and that we, as liberal Jews, bear a "responsibility to the Covenant Community." [23] That the *Halakhah* is pluralistic is amply borne out by the sources examined in this paper. Different stances concerning the possibility of retroactively annulling a conversion are certainly evident in the sources and authorities that have been examined. As liberal Jews, we need not adopt an approach on this issue that Rabbi Gunther Plaut has described as one in which "we begin with the Tradition and ask: how does it treat this *sheelah*. We then proceed to ask: What is there in our Liberal tradition that would have us disagree?"[24] In this instance, we need not dissent from the Tradition. The traditional *Halakhah* is sufficiently broad and pluralistic to encompass a liberal position on the matter.

That position, in light of R. Zemer's notion that a liberal *Halakhah* should both embody the ethical and reflect responsibility to the entire Covenantal Community, ought to be one that is consonant with the position put forth in the rabbinic sources cited in the first section of this paper, as well as the sentiments expressed by *halakhic* authorities such as Rabbis Kook, Unterman, and Uziel. They are surely more suitable as guides for our own policies in these matters than are the prescriptions advanced by *halakhists* such as Rabbis Ozer and Wiedenfeld. As R. Elliot Dorff, our Conservative colleague, and Arthur Dorsett, Professor of Law at the University of California at Los Angeles, have observed: "Emphasis on intention can cause more problems than it solves. Part of that problem is evidentiary: How does one prove an actor's intention? ... Intention is a slippery concept, for often our intentions are unclear, inconsistent, or misguided."[25]

To take the position adopted by the rabbis discussed and analyzed in the middle section of this paper would mean that no conversion could ever be fully established as legally valid. It would lead converts to never feel fully at home, fully confident of their status as Jews, for who could predict that no challenge to their Jewishness, no matter how observant they were, would be forthcoming. As Rabbi Saltzman has phrased it, "No convert would ever feel safe from the prying eyes of those who are looking for any excuse to void [a] conversion."[26] Furthermore, our age is marked by a denominationally-divided Jewish community where even rabbis within a specific branch of Judaism have radically different orientations towards and judgments concerning what constitutes "authentic Judaism." Any attempt to establish a single standard of *qabbalat ol mitzvot*, and to assert that proselytes who fail to fulfill that standard are not to be considered Jews, would mire the Jewish people in a morass of division and strife from which we could never be extricated.

Our movement would do well to follow the lead of the preponderance of talmudic sources on this issue for the reasons just stated. Retroactive annulment of conversion - except in the most extreme instances of fraud such as the case that came before the Law Committee of the Rabbinical Assembly - is a mine-field we ought to avoid on both pragmatic and moral-religious grounds. It will not serve a diverse and pluralistic Jewish people well in our day. Indeed, we should heed the sentiments of the late Rabbi Isaac Klein, who, on a parallel matter, observed so eloquently, "[In regard to the acceptance of conversion], we should not be overscrupulous. To follow the ways of peace and for the betterment of the world, we should ... not cause division in the House of Israel."[27]

Notes

1. Shlomo Goren, *P'sak hadin b'inyan haah v'ha-ahot*, Jerusalem, 5733-1973, p. 31-33.

2. Ibid., p. 32.

3. Ibid., pp. 150-152.

4. Ibid., p. 153.

5. Ibid., p. 8.

6. I would like to thank my colleague and friend, Rabbi Elliot Dorff, for sharing Rabbi Saltzman's responsum, as well as Rabbi Shapiro's dissent, with me. They will be published in the near future. The quotations here are taken from p. 10 of R. Saltzman's typescript and p. 3 of Rabbi Shapiro's.

7. Saul Lieberman, *Tosefta Kifeshuta*, p. 69.

8. *Teshuvot L'Rav Yehudai*, in B. Levin, ed., *Otzar HaGeonim, Masekhet Shabbat*, p. 128.

9. *Ezrat Kohen*, #13.

10. Ibid., #14.

11. *Hazon Nahum*, #90.

12. Chaim Ozer Grodzinsky, *Ahiezer: Kovetz Iggerot*, Vol. 1, B'nai B'rak, 1970, p. 75.

13. Abraham Dov Baer Kahane Shapira, "Conversion and Civil Marriage," *Talpiyot* 2:1, pp. 6-7.

14. Joel Roth, *The Halakhic Process: A Systematic Analysis*, New York, 1986, p. 253.

15. *Helkat Yaakov*, #13.

16. *Heihal Yitzhaq, Even HaEzer* I, #20.

17. Responsa of R. Isaac Halevi Herzog, *Yoreh Deah* 4, #92.

18. *Even Haezer* 3:4.

19. Isser Yehuda Unterman, "Laws of Conversion and Their Application," *Noam* (5731), pp. 5ff.

20. *Piskei Uziel*, 61, Cited by Moshe Ish-Horowicz, "The Case of Mrs. Paula Cohen and Her Children," *Newsletter of The Jewish Law Association* (November, 1991), p. 6.

21. *Mishpetei Uziel, Yoreh Deah*, #13.

22. Ibid., #14.

23. Moshe Zemer, "Authority and Criteria in Liberal Halakhah," in Walter Jacob and Moshe Zemer, eds., *Dynamic Jewish Law -- Progressive Halakhah*, Pittsburgh and Tel Aviv, 1991.

24. W. Gunther Plaut, "Reform Responsa as Liberal Halakhah," *Ibid.*, p. 116.

25. Elliot Dorff and Arthur Rosett, *A Living Tree: The Roots and Growth of Jewish Law*, Albany, 1988, pp. 53-54.

26. Steve Saltzman, "Annulment of a Conversion," p. 9.

27. Isaac Klein, *A Guide to Jewish Religious Practice*, New York, 1979, p. 447.

SINCERE CONVERSION AND ULTERIOR MOTIVES

Bernard M. Zlotowitz

From the beginning of the *Talmudic* period, rabbis have tended to discourage prospective converts to Judaism. However, in cases where the sincerity of the individual was not in doubt, they welcomed and embraced the candidate. In contrast, where the candidate's motives and sincerity are suspect, the attitude of the rabbis was ambivalent. In this paper we will examine the issue of a candidate's sincerity and ulterior motives as a determining factor in their admission to the Jewish faith and people.

The restrictive posture towards proselytes is a diaspora phenomenon, dictated primarily by hostile forces and/or the Jewish communities sense of security.[1] When Jews were the dominant force in society, however, they engaged in forcible conversion of heathens.[2]

The Bible does not talk about conversion. Therefore, no mention is made of sincerity or ulterior motives. The Story of Ruth's "conversion" is a rabbinic interpretation[3] of her statement to her mother-in-law: "Entreat me not to leave thee; for wither thou goest, I will go; and wither thou lodgest, I will lodge; thy people shall be my people, and thy God my God; where thou diest, will I die, and there will I be buried...."[4]

The earliest historical record we have of conversion to Judaism is the forcible conversion of the Idumeans by John Hyrcanus (135-104 B.C.E.), who gave them the choice between acceptance of Judaism or exile. They chose the former alternative to the disaster of the Jewish people. According to Graetz, "It was through the Idumeans and the Romans that the Hasmonean dynasty was overthrown and the Judaean State destroyed."[5] This tragedy of forced conversion was indelibly marked in the minds of the rabbis. Though they continued to proselytize, they were never truly enthusiastic about it. The rabbis placed obstacles in the way of a candidate for conversion.

In the Hellenistic Period, non-Jews were attracted to Judaism as a result of the Maccabean victory. But these non-Jews did not formally convert. They accepted the moral and ethical teachings of Judaism and the concept of one God. Josephus mentioned that many non-Jews observed the Sabbath.[6]

It has often been assumed that the royal family of Adiabene, on the Tigris River, during the Hellenistic Period converted to Judaism. However, it is likely that although Queen Helena (30 C.E.) converted, her son, Izates, did not. Izates did not undergo circumcision for fear of revolt by his people if they discovered they were being ruled by a Jew.[7]

Based on these few examples we can not determine whether ulterior motives were taken into account when a conversion took place. Likewise the historical account does not tell us how Jews reacted to those who took on some aspects of Judaism without fully converting. In all probability those that did convert were sincere in seeking to worship the one true God, though the stimulus might have been dubious.

It is really the *Talmud* and Codes that give us a true insight into whether ulterior motives were an important factor in accepting converts. The rabbis' attitude in this regard was ambivalent. They discussed, in great detail, whether or not one should be accepted for conversion for the sake of marriage, status (economic and/or social), out of fear, or the desire to take part in the Passover celebrations.

Individual rabbis differed in their degree of discouragement of *gerim*.[8] Rabbi Helbo, however, had disdain for them: "Proselytes are as difficult for Israel as leprosy."[9] This statement, cited to support the view that proselytes should not be accepted, has been misinterpreted. Rabbi Helbo merely conveyed a concern that the exceptional piety of proselytes embarrasses born Jews, and therefore is troublesome. Another antagonistic view was expressed by Maimonides that proselytes will not be received in the days of the Messiah.[10] However, these were not the prevailing views. Eliezer ben Pedat believed that Israel was dispersed for the purpose of gaining proselytes."[11] According to the *Mehilta*, Jethro wrote to Moses asking him to make it easy for people to convert to Judaism,[12] so that the "door was not shut in the face of the heathen."[13] In fact this became the *halakhic* view.

According to Jewish law there are four requirements for conversion: (1) acceptance of the Torah; (2) circumcision for males; (3) immersion; and (4) a sacrifice (which was discontinued after the destruction of the Temple). Beyond these requirements a major issue that occupied the rabbis was the motive of the convert in seeking to embrace Judaism.

The rabbis wanted the proselyte to have the same experience in receiving the Torah as did the Israelites at Mt. Sinai because this was the only way he/she could identify fully with Judaism. "Rabbi [Judah the Prince] says: Just as Israel did not enter the covenant except by means of three things - circumcision, immersion, and the acceptance of a sacrifice - so is it the same with proselytes." [14]

Circumcision was certainly required of the male convert, not only because of its covenantal implications, but as a sign of his good faith - his sincerity.

Unlike Christian baptism, immersion was for the purpose of purification, not initiation.[15]

Thus in viewing the individual convert, the rabbis drew a parallel to the Israelites entering into the covenant at Mt. Sinai - just as the Jew "was circumcised shortly before eating of the first paschal lamb, was immersed and offered sacrifices in preparation for the giving of the Torah at Mt. Sinai,"[16] so must the convert go through the same process.

The conversion process and ceremony was described in detail in the *Talmud*:

"Our Rabbis taught: If at the present time a man desires to become a proselyte, he is to be addressed as follows: 'what reason have you for desiring to become a proselyte; do you not know that Israel at the present time is persecuted and oppressed, despised, harassed and overcome by afflictions'? If he replies, 'I know and am unworthy', he is accepted forthwith, and is given instruction in some of the minor and some of the major commandments. He is informed of the sin [of the neglect of the commandments of] Gleanings, the Forgotten Sheaf, the Corner and the Poor Man's Tithe. He is also told of the punishment for the transgression of the commandments. Furthermore, he is addressed thus: 'Be it known to you that before you came to this condition, if you had eaten suet [forbidden fat] you would not have been punishable with *karet*, if you had profaned the Sabbath you would not have been punishable with stoning; but now were you to eat suet you would be punished with *karet*; were you to profane the Sabbath you would be punished with stoning'. And as he is informed of the punishment for the transgression of the commandments, so is he informed of the reward granted for their fulfillment. He is told, 'Be it known to you that the world to come was made only for the righteous, and that Israel at the present time are unable to bear either too much prosperity, or too much suffering? He is not, however, to be persuaded or dissuaded too much. If he accepted, he is circumcised forthwith. Should any shreds which render the circumcision invalid remain, he is to be circumcised a second time. As soon as he is healed, arrangements are made for his immediate ablution when two learned men must standby his side and acquaint him with some of the minor commandments and some of the major ones. When he comes up after his ablution he is deemed to be an Israelite in all respects.

"In the case of a woman proselyte, women make her sit in the water up to her neck, while two learned men stand outside and give her instruction in some of the minor commandments and some of the major ones....

"The Master said, 'If a man desires to become a proselyte...he is to be addressed as follows: "What reason have you for desiring to become a proselyte..." and he is made acquainted with some of the minor, and with some of the major commandments'. What is the reason? - In order that if he desires to withdraw, let him do so; for R. Helbo said: Proselytes are as hard for Israel [to endure] as a sore because it is written in Scripture," And the proselyte shall join himself with them, and they shall cleave to the house of Jacob" (Is.14.1).

"He is informed of the sin [of the neglect of the commandment of] Gleanings, the Forgotten Sheaf, the Corner and the Poor Man's Tithe'. What is the reason? - R. Hiyya b. Abba replied in the name of R. Johanan: Because a Noahide [idolaters] would rather be killed than spend so much as a *perutah* which is not returnable.

"He is not, however, to be persuaded or dissuaded too much! R. Eleazar said: what is the Scriptural proof? - it is written", And when she saw that she was steadfastly minded to go with her, she left off speaking to her" (Ruth 1.18). 'We are forbidden', she [Naomi] told her [Ruth], '[to move on the Sabbath beyond the] Sabbath boundaries'! - 'Whither thou goest' [the other replied] 'I will go'

"We are forbidden private meeting between man and woman!' Where thou lodgest, I will lodge.'

"We have been commanded six hundred and thirteen commandments!' 'Thy people shall be my people."

"We are forbidden idolatry!' - 'And thy God my God."

Four modes of death were entrusted to *Bet Din*!' -

'Where thou diest, will I die!'

Two graveyards [one for the worst offenders who suffered the death penalties of stoning or burning, and another for such as were executed by decapitation or strangulation] were placed at the disposal of the *Bet Din*!

-'And there will I be buried'. Presently "she saw that she was steadfastly minded, etc."

'If he accepted, he is circumcised forthwith? What is the reason? The performance of a commandment must not in any be delayed....

"When he comes up after his ablution he is deemed to be an Israelite in all respects? In respect of what practical issue? In that if he retracted and then betrothed the daughter of an Israelite he is regarded as a non-conforming Israelite and his betrothal is valid."[31]

The tractate *Yevamot* provided a list of motives to be taken into account: Sincerity, acceptance of all Toraitic laws[32] and a readiness to identify fully with the Jewish people through thick or thin.

SINCERE CONVERSION AND ULTERIOR MOTIVES

The question of motives is illuminated through a discussion between *Bet Hillel* and *Bet Shammai* on the status of a Jew just converted. They disagree over whether a proselyte converted on the 14th of *Nisan*, the day the Paschal lamb is slaughtered, was permitted to eat the Paschal lamb that evening. Hillel said he may not eat the Paschal lamb that evening because he has to wait a week to be cleansed from his impurity, just as anyone who becomes ritually impure from touching a corpse. Shammai, on the other hand, disagreed. Shammai did not consider the conversion as being a separation from a state of impurity to a status of purity:

"If a proselyte converted on the day before Passover, the House of Shammai says: He immerses and eats his paschal offering in the evening. But the House of Hillel says: One who departs from [his] foreskin is [as impure] as one departs from a grave."[33]

In another *Mishnah* we find support for *Bet Shammai*'s view: "Rabbi Eliezer ben Jacob says: There were soldiers and gatekeepers in Jerusalem who immersed and ate the paschal offerings in the evening."[34]

Rabbi Eliezer ben Jacob's statement is of exceptional interest. He stated that Roman soldiers who converted on the 14th of *Nisan* could eat the paschal lamb even though their motive may have solely been to participate in the Passover festivities because they were attracted to the beauty of the celebrations.

However, *Bet Shammai*'s view is not the prevailing one. The *Talmud*[35] emphasizes the need to reject those candidates for conversion with ulterior motives: for marriage, for love, or out of fear.

In a commentary[36] to the *Mishnah*, love is defined as "liking a particular person;" i.e. prefers to be in that person's company.

Fear refers to a situation in which gentiles, feeling threatened by Jews, would protect themselves by converting to the dominant faith. The *Mishnah* elucidates by recording the opinions of Rabbis Judah and Nehemiah that all those who converted in the days of Mordecai and Esther were not valid proselytes because they embraced Judaism only out of fear of reprisals by the Jews.

Thus those who do not convert for Heaven's sake (*l'shem shamayim*) are not acceptable as proselytes.

Maimonides repeated the *Mishnah*'s apprehension in accepting converts for ulterior motives and adds a few of his own:

"For financial gain, or to qualify for a position of authority,...or a woman [who]...has cast her eye upon one of the youths of Israel."[37]

So concerned was Maimonides over accepting converts for ulterior motives that he went into a lengthy discourse about the dangers of embarking on such a course. He blamed Samson and Solomon for the idolatry existing in the land. Had they not married heathen women who converted for ulterior motives, that evil would not have swept through the land of Israel:

"It should not be imagined that Samson, the deliverer of Israel, or Solomon, King of Israel, who was called 'the beloved of the Lord,' married foreign women while these were still heathens. Rather, the essence of the matter is as follows: The proper procedure, when a man or a woman comes forth with the intention of becoming a proselyte, is to examine them; perchance they come to embrace the faith in order to gain money, or to qualify for a position of authority, or out of apprehension. In the case of a man, perchance he has cast his eye upon an Israelite woman. In the case of a woman, it may be that she has cast her eye upon one of the youths of Israel. If no such ulterior motive is found in them, they should be informed of the heavy weight of the yoke of the Torah, and how burdensome it is for Gentiles to observe its precepts, in order to induce them to withdraw. If they accept the yoke nevertheless, and refuse to withdraw, and it is evident that they have forsaken heathenism out of love for the Torah, they should be accepted, as it is said: 'And when she saw that she was steadfastly minded to go with her, she left off speaking unto her' (Ruth 1.18).

"Consequently the court did not receive any proselytes throughout the days of David and Solomon; in the days of David, lest they should become proselytes out of apprehension and in Solomon's time, lest they should become proselytes on account of the might, the prosperity, and the greatness which Israel then enjoyed. For whosoever forsakes heathenism for the sake of some worldly vanity is not considered a righteous proselyte. Nevertheless, many became proselytes in the presence of laymen during the days of David and Solomon; and the Great Court was apprehensive on that account. While the court did not repulse them, at any rate after they had immersed themselves, neither did it welcome them, until such time as their subsequent conduct could be observed.

"Now since Solomon caused the women to become proselytes first, before marrying them - and so did Samson - and it is a known fact that these women had become proselytes for ulterior motives; and since Samson and Solomon made them proselytes without the sanction of the court, therefore Scripture regarded them as heathens remaining in their state of prohibition. Moreover, their later activity showed the true reason for their former ones, for they continued to worship their idols and built high places for them, which is why Scripture holds Solomon responsible as though he built them himself, as it is said: 'Then did Solomon build a high place' (I Kings 11.7).

"A proselyte who has not undergone an examination, or was not made acquainted with the commandments and the punishment for transgressing them, but was circumcised and immersed in the presence of three laymen, is deemed a proselyte. Even if it becomes known that he had become a proselyte because of some ulterior motive, once he is circumcised and immersed, he has left the status of a heathen, but apprehension should be felt concerning him until his righteousness shall have become apparent. Even if he reverts to his previous state and worships idols, he is considered merely a renegade Israelite, his act of betrothal remains valid, and it remains the finder's duty to return to him his lost property, for once a person immerses himself, he attains the status of an Israelite. That is why Samson and Solomon kept their wives, even though their secret motives were revealed.

"It is for this reason that the Sages have declared, 'Proselytes are as hard to bear for Israel as a scab upon the skin,' since the majority of them become proselytes for ulterior motives and subsequently lead Israel astray, and once they become proselytes, it is a difficult matter to separate from them. An instructive example is what happened in the wilderness in the matter of the golden calf...as well as in most of the trials with which Israel wearied God. All of these were initiated by the mixed multitude."[38]

There is basically no difference in attitude expressed in Jacob ben Asher's *Turim - Yoreh Deah*.[39] or in Joseph Caro's *Shulhan Arukh - Yoreh Deah*.[40]

Despite the *Talmud*'s and the Codes' viewpoints that impure motives would be sufficient ground to deny an individual the rite of conversion, we do have examples to the contrary.

Hillel and Rabbi Hiya accepted converts even though the candidates' motives were not of the purest. Hillel converted a man who wanted to become High Priest[41] and Rabbi Hiya converted a woman who fell in love with a student.[42]

SINCERE CONVERSION AND ULTERIOR MOTIVES

Though Hillel and Rabbi Hiya did allow conversions, for ulterior motives, the *Shulhan Arukh - Yoreh Deah* solidified the view that ulterior motives were to be rejected, if the *Bet Din* so determined.[43]

In developing a modern perspective on this issue, we should turn to Shammai, the examples cited by Hillel and Rabbi Hiya and the liberal view advanced by Rabbi David Zvi Hoffman. Rabbi Hoffman wrote a responsum relating to a situation in which a Jewish woman is married by civil law to a non-Jew. Later the non-Jewish partner seeks to convert which Rabbi Hoffman sanctions despite the candidate's ulterior motives (i.e. love of his wife). To support his decision, Rabbi Hoffman cites the examples of Hillel and Rabbi Hiya.

"The *Shulhan Arukh* rules that we do not accept as a proselyte one who wishes to convert in order to marry a Jew. However, the *Tosafot* has already raised an objection to this position based on the incident of Hillel who converted the gentile who wanted to become *high priest*, as well as that of R. Hiya, who accepted a woman who had fallen in love with a student. The *Tosafot* resolved the difficulty by saying that the rabbis were convinced that these proselytes would eventually become Jews for the sake of Heaven. The codifiers cited this, and they learned from it that in matters of conversion, the decision was left to the discretion of the rabbinical court. If the court was convinced that a proselyte is religiously sincere, even though he has fallen in love with a Jewish woman, he may be accepted.

"Now in our case, since the gentile in question has already married a Jewish woman under civil law...it is clear that she will remain his wife if he does not convert. Thus, we have reason to believe that his request for conversion is based upon sincere motivations. Moreover, if we do not accept him, she will remain with him in spite of the Toraitic prohibition against Jewish-Gentile marital relations. If so, it is better to accept him than allow her to remain in a sinful relationship.

"If you should object: how can we allow the court to sin (by accepting an insincere proselyte) in order to save this woman from a sin? We might reply that her children from this man who will be Jews according to *halakhah*, might very well be drawn to their father's religion. If this happens, they will become transgressors (apostates) through no fault of their own, and 'these lambs, what is their sin?

"It is, therefore, better for the court to choose the lesser evil, accept this proselyte, educate him in Judaism, and insure that his children will be raised as Jews. At any rate, it should adjure him to observe the precepts of Judaism, in particular those relating to *Shabbat* and *kashrut*, and receive the affirmation to do so."[44]

This view should serve as our guide that whoever wishes to convert and for whatever reason should be accepted. So long as they renounce their former religion, accept the uniqueness of the God of Israel, are willing to circumcise their male children, cast their lot with the Jewish people, we should encourage them and embrace them. The psychological trauma of leaving a religion in which one was reared is very profound. If a person is willing to undertake such a step, which is not easy, let us stretch out our hand to him/her and to welcome them, after proper study and preparation, into the Household of Judaism.

In fact, this is the message the Central Conference of American Rabbis was sending us when they voted in the convention assembled in 1891, at the urging of Isaac Mayer Wise, not to insist on *b'rit milah* for adult converts.

Today, upwards of ninety percent of conversions are due to marriage. Though many wish to come to Judaism because they are going to marry a Jew, "The outcome has shown that the conversion, although occasioned by an ulterior motive, was neither perfunctory nor insincere."[45] Shall we turn potential Jews away because the *halakhah* deems marriage as a reason for conversion invalid? Whether these converts become devoted and dedicated Jews is primarily our responsibility. We need to encourage the convert to continue studying Judaism, participate in the life of the synagogue and the Jewish community. In this way, we ensure that the convert will then become one with our people - in mind, body and soul.

Notes

A special thanks to Rabbis Alan S. Kaplan, Gary Bretton-Granatoor and Mr. Aron Hirt-Manheimer for their invaluable suggestions in the preparation of this paper.

1. Two examples: (1) Hadrianic persecutions; (2) Christian edicts forbidding conversion to Judaism.

2. See example below.

3. *b. Yevamot* 47b

4. Ruth 1.16, 17. Ruth's plea to her mother-in-law was an expression of her strong desire to stay with Naomi. Ruth's acceptance of God did not necessarily signal a renunciation of her other gods. From my view-point, Ruth was not a convert to Judaism. Similarly, Solomon built a shrine for Chemosh, the god of Moab (I K 11.1,7), so that his Moabitish wives could worship the pagan god, even though they supposedly had "converted" to Judaism. Thus, like Solomon's wives, Ruth did not embrace the Jewish God exclusively. The Book of Ruth was written to oppose Ezra's decree that foreign wives be cast out. Had Judaism adhered to Ezra's decree, the author(s) of the Book of Ruth argue that there never would have been a King David as Ruth was his ancestress (Harry M. Orlinsky, *Understanding the Bible Through History and Archaeology*, KTAV, 1972, pp. 236 and 238). Bernard Bamberger argues that the Bible implicitly supports proselytism. He bases his opinion on Isaiah's message of a universal God (*The Universal Jewish Encyclopedia*, vol. 9, p. 3). Such an interpretation reflects a modern perspective absent during the Biblical period. The prophets were not interested in the non-Jew except when it involved the welfare of the Jewish people. "The prophets were concerned directly and exclusively with this 'chosen people,' and they took notice of other peoples only when the latter came into contact...with Judah and Israel (Harry M. Orlinsky, *Op. Cit.*, p. 268). Furthermore, Bamberger's reference that the reaction against Ezra's decrees in casting

out non-Jewish wives is indicated in the Book of Ruth is correct (*Op. Cit.*). However, the Book of Ruth is not talking about proselytization but about intermarriage; i.e. marriage between a Jew and a non-Jew.

5. Heinrich Graetz, *History of the Jews*, Philadelphia, 1946, Vol. 2, p. 9.

6. *Against Apion*, Book 2, chap. 39.

7. *Antiquities* xx, ii, 4 (34-38).

8. Though the rabbis distinguished between *ger toshav* and *ger tzedeq*, we will confine ourselves to the term *ger*, proselyte.

9. *b. Yevamot* 47b, 109b; *Kid.* 70b; *Avodah Zarah* 3b; *Ket.* 11a; *Niddah* 13b.

10. Yad, *Hil. Issurei Biah*, 13-14. See also *Yoreh Deah* 268.

11. *b. Pesahim* 87b.

12. *Yitro, Amalek*, 3.

13. *Pesiqta Rabbati* 35, quoted in *Jewish Encyclopedia*, vol.10, p. 222.

14. *Sifrei Bamidbar*, 108.

15. See Lawrence H. Schiffman, *Who Was a Jew?*, New York, 1985, p. 26. Schiffman contends that immersion may also have been seen as an initiatory rite. I doubt this because immersion was regarded, *halakhically*, as a means of purification; e.g. *nidah*.

16. *Ibid*, p. 19.

31. *b. Yevamot* 47 a & b. Soncino translation.

32. See also *Demai* 2.5.

33. *b. Pesahim* 8.8.

34. *M. Pesahim* 7.14. See also *b. Pesahim* 92a, where this story of Roman soldiers is attributed to Rabbi Simeon ben Elazar.

35. *Gerim* 1.7.

36. *Nahalat Yaakov* on 1.7 in Gerim.

37. *Yad*, Hil. Issurei Biah 13.14.

38. *Ibid.*, 13.14-18.

39. Chapters 268 ff.

40. Chapters 267 ff.

41. *b. Shabbat* 31a.

42. *b. Menahot* 44a.

43. Chapters 268-269.

44. *Responsum Melamed Le-Ho'il*, #83, Cited by Rabbi Mark Washofsky at the study session of the Commission on Reform Jewish Outreach, October 31, 1991, Baltimore, MD.

45. Bernard Bamberger, *The Universal Jewish Encyclopedia*, Vol. 9, p.3. Though written many years ago, its words are as true today as they were then.

AMBIVALENCE IN PROSELYTISM

Moshe Zemer

Eight hundred years ago, a Palestinian rabbi humiliated a proselyte by denigrating the allegedly idolatrous practices of his Muslim ancestors. The convert, R. Obadiah Ger Zedek, complained to Maimonides, who reprimanded the rabbi and warned him that the Torah commands us treat the proselyte with tenderness and understanding.[1]

Eight centuries have passed and we still find that prospective converts are treated badly by official rabbinical establishments in many parts of the world. In certain countries, a candidate must traverse an arduous obstacle course before conversion. In others, rabbinic courts have stopped converting altogether.

Conversion for an Ulterior Motive

One key to the ambivalent attitude towards converts is the principle requirement for conversion, *kabbalat ol hamitzvot*, the sincere acceptance of the religion of Israel and its precepts. The early *halakhah* forbade conversion to Judaism for ulterior motives such as marriage.

A second century sage, R. Nehemiah, ruled that a man who became a proselyte for the sake of a woman and a woman who converted for the wake of a man, (or for any other extraneous reason) are not proselytes. However, later *Talmudic halakhah* determined in the name of the third century Amora, Rab, that even if they converted to Judaism because of an ulterior motive, nonetheless, *bediavad* (*post factum*) they are valid Jewish converts.[2]

However, as we shall see, this prohibition was frequently circumvented. Not long before the Spanish Expulsion, Rabbi Shelomo b. Shimon Duran (Rashbash, 1400-1467) of Algeria, was asked about conversion of the *conversos* (Marranos) and their descendants to Judaism. In his responsum, he quotes the accepted *halakhah* that it is forbidden to accept a person who wishes to convert to Judaism for any kind of ulterior motive. Nevertheless, the Rashbash, claimed that "this prohibition applies only to a *goi*, (i.e., a gentile without Jewish ancestors) who wishes to convert. However, if the candidate is one of the *anusim* (Marranos) or their descendants, we do not reject them because or an ulterior motive. Rather, it is our obligation to draw them near and bring them under the wings of the *shekhinah* (the Diving Presence)."[3]

The *Tosafot*[4] query: If conversion may not be allowed for an ulterior motive, how could Hillel the Elder have accepted the person who came to him with the demand: "Convert me so that I might be High Priest."[5] These *Talmudic* commentators answer that Hillel was certain that this gentile could eventually convert for the sake of Heaven. This was also the case of the Roman courtesan who wished to convert to Judaism in order to marry a *yeshivah* student of the third century Palestinian Amora, Rabbi Hiyya, the head of the academy, who accepted her because he was positive that she would become a sincere convert.[6]

How can one determine the intent, *kavannah* of the prospective convert to accept fully a Jewish way of life, the key to a sincere, valid conversion. How may we validate the candidate's sincerity, which is a "matter of the heart," part of his/her inner being, thoughts and conscience that are not readily apparent. R. Joseph Caro tells us that it is one of the responsibilities and powers of the Rabbinical Court to judge whether the candidate will indeed become a sincere convert to Judaism and concludes: "You must learn that everything depends upon the judgement of the *Bet Din*."[7]

Negative Views

In contrast with these affirmative attitudes to conversion, we hear the proclamation of the Amorah, R. Isaac: "Evil after evil comes upon those who receive proselytes... (which is deduced from a statement) of R. Helbo, who said: *kashim gerim le-yisrael k'sapahat* - proselytes are as difficult to Israel as a skin disease.[8]

Why does evil come upon those who accept converts and why are they such a burden to Israel? Several explanations are given:

(a) A *tosafist*, Rabbi Isaac (b. Shmuel the Elder), explained that the warning about accepting converts refers to those gentiles who were enticed to convert, or were received immediately without any requirements. However, if gentiles exert themselves to convert, we must receive them.[9]

(b) Another explanation of the difficulty that proselytes cause born Jews is God's warning in twenty-four (or some say thirty-six) places in Scripture that forbids us not to wrong converts. It is impossible for us to fulfill all of these commandments and not to grieve them. [10]

(c) Others say that converts are responsible for Israel's dispersion through the diaspora as the *Talmud* comments: "Why is Israel dispersed among all of the nations more than are the gentiles? In order that proselytes be added to them."[11]

(d) Rashi said that the difficulty with *gerim* is that they are not careful in their observance of *mitzvot* so born Jews who associate with converts are attracted to their ways and learn from their deeds.[12]

(e) In contrast, a *Tosafist*, R. Abraham the Proselyte claimed: Since converts are expert in *mitzvot* and are punctilious with them, they are as difficult to Israel as a skin disease, because as a result, God reminds the Jews of their sins when they are not doing His will.[13]

We should note the inconsistencies in these views. On the one hand converts cause born Jews difficulties because they are not careful in the observance of commandments and on the other hand because they are expert in the *mitzvot* and punctilious in their observance. The socio-religious character of these complaints reflect the problems on converts interacting with born Jews.

In Praise of Proselytes

In contrast with this denigration of converts, we find almost unlimited praise in *tannaitic* sources. The *Mekhilta* declares: "Beloved are the proselytes - (*havivim gerim*) and proceeds to bring more than twenty Scriptural precedents requiring us to treat them with loving care.

The rabbis found the proof text for the appropriate behavior towards a proselyte: "'You shall not wrong a *ger*, neither shall you oppress him, for you were *gerim* in the Land of Egypt' - You shall not wrong him - with words. Neither shall you oppress him - in money matters"(*Exodus* 22.28). The *Mekhilta* then proceeds to warn us not to remind the proselyte of his pagan past.[14]

Jewish tradition presents us with contradicting statements of praise and condemnation of proselytes. Are these merely the individual opinions of various *Tannaim* and *Amoraim*, or are these *halakhic* statements which obligate ensuing generations?

The *Mitzvah* of Accepting Converts

Whether the rabbis found converts helpful or harmful to Israel, may be related to their view of a crucial issue: Is the acceptance of a non-Jew into Judaism a matter of the predilection of the individual rabbi or *Bet Din* or is it a *mitzvah* to accept candidates for conversion and to bring them into the Jewish fold? Indeed, are we commanded to convert gentiles to Judaism?

Maimonides informs us in his Book of the Commandments that the verse: "'And you shall love the Lord your God' (Deuteronomy 5:5)... commands us to seek out and call upon all humankind to serve God and to believe in him... and when you truly love God... you undoubtedly search for unbelievers and the unlearned and bring them to knowledge of the truth which you have acquired."[15]

The Rambam goes on to quote the *Sifre* on Deuteronomy: "'And you shall love (*ve-ahavtah*) the Lord your God... make him beloved (*ahavehu*) by all his creatures as did Abraham your father... "Just as Abraham loved God... and with his great understanding and faith sought out people (and led them) to the faith strengthened in his love, so shall you love God until you seek out and call mankind unto Him."[16]

Some commentators explain Maimonides' interpretation of this commandment as a call to receive converts and bring them into the fold, even though he did quote the rest of the *Sifre* commentary on Abraham: "This teaches that Abraham, our father, converted them and brought them under the wings of the Divine Presence."[17]

An eleventh century sage, R. Isaac ben Reuben of Barcelona, lists the conversion of gentiles as a positive commandment derived from another verse: "And you shall love the *ger*" (Deut. 10:19). he proclaims in poetic verse: "The proselyte who comes to be converted shall take refuge with you. When he says to you: I shall take shelter with you, the (members of the *Bet Din*) will accept him and inform him of some of the light and stringent commandments. Lest he change his mind and say 'What have I done? I cannot go with these, for I am not used to them.'" (I Samuel 17:39)[18]

R. Shimon bar Zemah Duran, (the Rashbatz, Spain, 1361-1444) exclaimed: "I am surprised that *qabbalat gerim* (the acceptance of converts) is not included in the list of commandments. It is indeed a *mitzvah* directed to the *Bet Din* to accept converts and not to reject them just as we learn in the *Talmud*: Once a proselyte has converted *immediately*, because 'the performance of a *mitzvah* must not in any way be delayed.'[19] This shows that the *Talmud* views conversion as a *mitzvah*." According to the Rashbatz, the acceptance of converts is a *mitzvah* incumbent upon a *Bet Din* and should be included in the list of *taryag ha-mitzvot* (the 613 commandments of the Torah). Since this precept cannot be derived from any other *mitzvah*, it should be listed as a separate commandment.[20]

These are but a few examples of *Talmudic* and medieval sources that reveal rabbinic ambivalence regarding conversion. We have noted that their views range from predicting peril to rabbis who accept converts to proclaiming that conversion is commanded by the Torah. To what extent are these ancient *halakhic* views of acceptance and rejection of *gerim* reflected in the approach to conversion in our modern era? We shall explore a few cases in modern responsa literature, which illustrate ambivalence in applying ancient *halakhah* to modern situations.

An Eternal Ban on Conversion

A radically negative approach to proselytes found its expression in a rabbinic ban against conversion promulgated almost seven decades ago in Argentina. This *takanah*, enacted in 1927 by

Rabbi Shaul David Setton (1851-1930), the spiritual leader of the Syrian Jewish community of Buenos Aires, prohibited even *halakhic* conversions under Orthodox auspices.[21] The prohibition covered all of Argentina "until the end of time" (*kol yemei olam*) and is, to a certain extent, still in effect today.[22]

The stated reason for forbidding conversions is "because life in this city (Buenos Aires) is exceedingly wanton, and everybody does as he pleases; there is no rabbi serving the Jewish community, whose authority is respected by the government or any other party." One of the co-sponsors of the decree was Rabbi Aharon Halevi Goldman (1854-1932), who provided its *halakhic* and ideological foundation. Goldman, an outstanding *Talmudic* scholar born in Russia, in 1889 became the founder and spiritual leader of the Jewish colony, Moisesville (*Kiryat Moshe*), located 600 kilometers north of Buenos Aires in the province of Santa Fe.

Goldman clearly states his view of the reason why Jewish men wish to have their gentile wives converted in Argentina:

> "I was startled to hear and alarmed to see" (Isaiah 21:3) the news of the state of affairs in the land, that there are men who have thrown off the yoke of Heaven. They have taken gentile wives and have begotten with them children. Then to cover up their wantonness, they wish to have their alien wives and foreign children accepted as converts to and included in the Congregation of Israel...Who would be such a fool as to be taken in by their declaration that they sincerely wish to convert their alien wives and foreign children, since all their trickery and deceit are nothing but an attempt to whitewash their irresponsibility, in order to obtain religious sanction.[23]

Setton who promulgated and executed the "eternal" ban was not always against conversion in his community. In 1915, about twelve years before the proclamation of the ban, Setton asked Goldman on behalf of a *Bet Din* in Buenos Aires requesting his help in the conversion of a Syrian Arab living in their community. Setton warmly recommended this prospective convert whose motivation is for the sake of heaven. "Our hopes are great that you will promptly do everything and even more...for it is known how great is the *mitzvah* (of conversion) and its reward."[24]

Goldman in his responsum states that it is impossible to accept proselytes in this country because, according to rabbinic sources,[25] one must inform the prospective convert in advance of some aspects of the punishment for the violation of commandments such as the desecrating of the Sabbath and eating forbidden foods.

> To my consternation, and that of every upright person, the scourge has spread here, for many of our brethren have abandoned the Torah, so that stringent *mitzvot* like the desecration of the Sabbath have become the lightest of the light. These violators so outnumber us, that if one should find a Jew who keeps the Shabbat and like, he would be considered on a level with a *tzaddik*. There are so few that a child could make a list.

> Now imagine, if we warn the convert concerning all the above (*mitzvot*) and afterwards when he sees with his own eyes, how many of our brothers trespass everything with contempt, then he will surely ask: what was all this that the Rabbis of Israel warned us, is not the House of Israel just like all the gentiles? Are we not then responsible when, God forbid, he vilifies all of the disciplines of Judaism...therefore I'll have nothing to do with this case.[26]

Goldman held an absolutist view. A non-Jew could not hope for a valid conversion, even if he/she were to fulfill all of the requirements of the rabbinic codes. The Rabbi of Moisesville insisted that converts be accepted only if they lived in a community with universal observance of the mitzvot. Of course, an environment of this sort was non-existent in the cities of Argentina of that time.

An absolutist is often known to demand the fulfillment of conditions and prerequisites that cannot be reasonably met. Even the finest candidate possible could not have been converted because there was no completely observant Jewish community such as Meah Shearim or Williamsburg where he could live in Argentina. Conversion is indeed permitted in the *Talmud*, and the rabbinic literature, Goldman could not abrogate it by fiat. However, by raising difficult *halakhic* obstacles, he effectively eliminated the possibility of conversion for those who accepted his authority.

This extremely stringent view of conversion led to the radical decree against conversions in all of the Argentine for all time. This ban did not just remain in South America, but was exported to the United States. The ban was adopted by the Syrian Jewish Community of Brooklyn, New York, in 1935, with the amendment that "no future Rabbinic Court will have the right or authority to convert non-Jews who seek to marry into our community." The Buenos Aires ban on all conversions for all Jews everywhere in Argentina was transformed into a prohibition on conversion for marriage in the Syrian Jewish community of the New York city borough. This ban was reconfirmed and signed by all the rabbis and lay leaders of the Syrian and Sephardic Jewish Communities with special warnings and proclamations in 1946, 1972, and 1984.[27]

The Ambivalent Chief Rabbi

Rabbi Mordecai Jacob Breisch, *Av Bet Din* of Zurich, proclaimed a ban on conversion in the mid 1940s: "We shall prohibit, *lehatkhilah* (*ab initio*) the acceptance of converts for the purpose of marriage".[28] Breish wrote to the Chief Rabbi of *Eretz Yisrael*, Isaac Herzog, requesting his support for the struggle of the Orthodox Community of Switzerland against conversion. Breisch published Herzog's 1947 responsum which fully justified *milhemet Hashem* (God's war) waged by Breisch and his Agudat Harabanim against conversion in Switzerland. Herzog spares no *halakhic* argument in opposing conversion for the sake of marriage:

> "Although the *halakhah* has determined that those who converted for ulterior motives and not for the sake of Heaven, are nevertheless proselytes *post factum*, I have a compelling reason to claim that this is not the law today. In the past, almost every Jew was constrained to observe the *mitzvot*, otherwise he would be rejected and held in contempt. This social situation strengthened the assumption that the gentile who has come to convert to Judaism, was truly resolved to kept the *Shabbat*, etc...but today the situation is different and it is possible to be a Jewish leader, while desecrating the *Shabbat* and eating forbidden foods in public. Therefore, how can we make the assumption that the gentile has resolved, even if only at the time of conversion, to observe Judaism? This is especially so, when the overwhelming majority, and perhaps all proselytes of this ilk, do not even begin to keep the fundamentals of our religion."[29]

Here we see an extremist view of conversion. Herzog is willing to re-interpret a lenient *Talmudic* ruling to justify the exclusion of prospective converts. David Ellenson analyzes the decisor's motivation as well as the sociological background of this responsum:

> "Herzog clearly viewed conversion in cases such as this as causing intermarriage rather than regarding them as a

logical outcome of social conditions where Jews and gentiles socially interacted with one another. Hence he felt these conversions attenuated the strength of Judaism in the contemporary setting...

Herzog's responsum obviously stands as a stringent interpretation of, and perhaps even expansion on, Jewish law in this field. It reflects the embattled position Orthodox rabbinic authorities perceived themselves as occupying vis-a-vis the non-observant Jewish community and, as such, it represents the ever-increasing polarity between Orthodox and non-Orthodox Jewries in the contemporary world."[30]

Ellenson shows here, as in his other works, that *halakhic* decisions cannot be understood in terms of rabbinic law alone, but must be studied in the framework of the sociological and organizational needs of the decisor and those whom he supports.[31]

In contrast with this extremist position, Herzog authored a very different responsum on this subject. He was asked about the validity of the conversion of a gentile woman, who was civilly married to a Jew. Could this woman have a Jewish marriage with her spouse? In a closely reasoned *teshuvah*, composed in 1941, the Chief Rabbi relies on a responsum by Maimonides, who permitted a man to manumit his female slave and marry her contrary to *Talmudic* law.[32] Herzog states that "according to the situation, there are times one should permit such prohibitions so that a Jew would not become mired in sin." Furthermore, he explains: "A great deal depends on the judgement of the decisor and his *kavannah* for the sake of Heaven." Herzog then goes on to give a lenient decision:

"If they were coming to ask whether to convert her or not, we would say: Convert her so that she may be married, for it is certain that they will not separate from one another, so that the (Jewish) man will remain in a permanent state of sin having marital relations with a non-Jewess...and since the conversion was permitted *ab initio*, it is obvious that they may have *huppah ve-qiddushin* (a Jewish wedding)."[33]

Herzog appears to be contradicting himself. How can we explain the diametrically opposite approaches to conversion in these two responsa? Did the Chief Rabbi change his mind in the six years between the two responsa? Was he more lenient in this 1941 case because it relates to a situation in the Land of Israel?

In the second section of this permissive responsum, Herzog changes his tone and writes in a prohibitive manner very similar to his letter to the Swiss rabbinic body:

"Albeit the *halakhah* is in accordance with those who say that they are all converts (*post factum*, even if they converted for an extraneous purpose), but nevertheless I am in doubt regarding such conversion in our day; because in the days of the Sages and the Decisors, of blessed memory, there was almost no room within the Congregation of Israel for a non-observant Jew. Therefore it was permissible to accept the promise of a convert to keep the *mitzvot*, even if there was a material motive for the conversion, because otherwise his existence was precarious. However, to our great distress, the situation is so riotous today that Jews according to the *halakhah* are among the most unobservant of Israel, and many of them are leaders of communities, and even leaders of our Nation...why should this gentile keep the commandments when so many Jews are not observant...the (convert's) acceptance of the *mitzvot* is doubtful when there is an ulterior motive for the conversion...we must therefore judge these persons to be doubtful proselytes. The law has changed when they come to us for conversion, so we must refuse them because...we would be allowing an admixture of the offspring of doubtful gentile in Israel."[34]

Apparently, Herzog's basically negative position on conversion for the sake of marriage did not change. He did, however, permit conversion and marriage under certain circumstances, finding other *halakhic* precedents to justify his decisions. However, he found it necessary to qualify his lenient decisions with the same caveat he sent to the Swiss rabbis.

This was not just a chance action on his part. In December 1948, the Chief Rabbi wrote another lenient responsum in which he permitted the conversion of gentile women married to Jews "not for the sake of Heaven, but for *aliyah* to the Land of Israel."[35] After finding *halakhic* bases for granting their request, Herzog once again appended an almost identical admonition about the severe dangers of accepting proselytes.[36]

Perhaps, one key to Herzog's ambivalent approach is in the identity of his questioners. The extremely Orthodox Aggudat Harabanim of Switzerland was seeking the Chief Rabbi's imprimatur and support of their holy war against conversion. Herzog was more than willing to repeat his declaration of dissociation from accepting proselytes. A rabbinic decisor may not always be an impartial judge, but rather an advocate who wishes to help colleagues involved in *halakhic* polemics. Responsa frequently involves advocacy.

In the cases of the anonymous convert of Palestine, who wished to marry a Jew, and the women who wanted to convert so they could come on *aliyah*, Herzog gave permissive responsa. In these cases he also gave the answers that the women and their rabbinic questioners wished to hear. Even though he was compelled to repeat his reservations about the *halakhic* validity of conversion, he could nonetheless find alternate justification in the wake of *halakhic* decisions rendered by decisors in the 19th and 20th centuries. In each of these responsa, both negative and positive, the questioner received the reply that was desired.

The Affirmative Approach to Conversion

In his permissive decisions, Herzog kept good company with decisors like R. Yaakov Yehiel Weinberg (the last *rosh yeshivah* of the Hildesheimer Rabbinical Seminary in Berlin) and others. These respondents stated that a gentile who is married civilly to a Jewish person, his or her desire to convert should not be construed as *giur leshem ishut*, conversion for the ulterior motive of marriage, because they are already living together and won't be separated if a conversion is refused.[37]

Many respondents found *halakhic* justification for conversion for the sake of marriage. The major cause for this change was the introduction of civil marriage after the Emancipation and the large number of Jews who were legally married to gentiles in the eyes of the State in which they lived. It was impossible to ignore this phenomenon which became one of the most serious issues of many Jewish communities.

The late Sephardic Chief Rabbi Ben Zion Uziel expressed a very positive view of a relationship of this kind: "This woman is already married to a Jew and when she enters the covenant of Judaism (*brit ha-yahadut*) she will become closer to her husband's family and to his Torah and furthermore the children who will be born to her will be full fledged Jews. This is just like the deeds of Hillel and R. Hiyya, who were certain that in the end they would be proper proselytes, and therefore it is a *mitzvah* to draw converts near and bring them into the covenant of Judaism."[38]

As we have seen, rabbinic sages throughout the ages were extremely concerned about the insincere convert. What happens if a rabbinic court makes a mistake in accepting a candidate for conversion? R. Eliyahu Gutmacher, *Av Bet Din* of Graditz (1796-1874), said that in a case where we are in doubt whether the candidate is sincere or not, every rabbi should prefer to accept the convert rather than reject him.

> "If it is not certain that the candidate is acting from an ulterior motive, we must accept him, because we would be more liable if we rejected him than if we accepted him as a convert without *halakhic* justification. For we shall see, if he misleads us by saying that he's converting for the sake of Heaven and he lied, and we accepted him on this basis, what's the big fuss? We found (in the *Talmud* and *Shulhan Arukh* that there were similar cases not for the sake of heaven), and the *Bet Din* knew it and transgressed and accepted them as converts, so that our candidate would be a full convert, and how much the more so, if the *Bet Din* concluded that they relied on his lie and thought that he told the truth there's no curse upon them."[39]

What is it that leads decisors to advocacy or opposition, acceptance or reaction of converts? It may be the individual rabbi's attitude toward gentiles in general. Perhaps the reason may be found in the way that a particular generation of Jews was treated. It is often the *Weltanschauung* (the world outlook) of the respondent which may be open and accepting as we find in the decisions of Hoffman and Uziel or hostile and excluding like the responsa of Goldman and Breisch. It may be a sincere belief that conversion is the *cause* rather than the result of intermarriage. Whatever the reason may be, there is most certainly a myriad of precedents to buttress whatever conclusion the respondent reaches.

Perhaps the most appropriate resolution of this issue may be found in Maimonides' responsum to R. Obadiah the Proselyte, which gives his appraisal of a sincere convert:

> "A person who has left his parents and birthplace and the sovereignty of his people, who are ruling, who by his understanding heart has joined a people that is so abused and persecuted, because he learned to...recognize that their religion represents truth and righteousness and recognized all this and followed after the Lord and entered beneath the wings of the Divine Presence...desiring His commandments and lifting up his heart to draw near to God in the light of the living...God calls him the disciple of Abraham our father who left his parents and birthplace and turned to the Lord."[40]

Notes

1. *Teshuvot HaRambam*, (ed. Jehoshua Blau), Jerusalem, 1986, v. 2, no. 448.

2. b. *Yevamot* 24b.

3. *Responsa HaRashbash*, Livorno, 1742, no. 368.

4. *Tosafot Yevamot* 24b, s.v. lo bimei David.

5. b. *Shabbat* 31a.

6. b. *Menahot* 44a.

7. *Bet Yosef, Yoreh Deah* 268. Cf. Shabbtai Cohen, Siftei Cohen ad loc 12 (23).

8. b. *Yevamot* 109b. Modern commentators believe that this is psoriasis, which is not dangerous, but a very bothersome disease which is difficult to cure. See *Encyclopedia Hebraica*, Jerusalem, 1974, v. 26, col. 766-767.

9. b. *Tosefot Yevamot* 109b, s.v. ra'ah.

10. b. *Tosefot Kiddushin* 70b, s.v. kashim.

11. b. *Pesachim* 7b.

12. b. *Kiddushin* 70b, s.v. *kashim*.

13. supra note 10.

14. *Mekhilta de-Rabbi Ishmael* (ed. Lauterbach+, Tractate *Neziqin*, Chapter 18, pp. 137-138. See supra note 1.

15. Maimonides, *Sefer HaMitzvot*, (ed. H. Heller), Positive Commandment no. 3.

16. *Sifrei Deuteronomy*, (ed. Meir Ish Halom), Vienna, 1864, sec. 32; (ed. Finkelstein), New York, 1969, sec. 32.

17. Yeruham Fischel Perla, *Commentary on Sefer HaMitzvot of Rabbi Sa'adya Gaon*, Warsaw, 1914, positive commandment no. 19, p. 295. See also *Talmudic Encyclopedia*, Jerusalem, 1975, vol. 1, col. 205 and vol. 6, col. 426.

18. *Sefer Derekh Mitzvotekhah (Azharot)*, Susa, Tunisia, 1920, p. 16.

19. b. *Yevamot* 47b.

20. *Zohar HaRaqia*, Constantinople, 1515, positive commandment no. 40.

21. See Moshe Zemer, "The Rabbinic Ban on Conversion in Argentina", *Judaism*, v. 37, no. 1, Winter, 1988, pp. 84-96.

22. Shaul David Setton, *Responsa Dibber Shaul*, Jerusalem, 1928, *Yoreh Deah* no. 3.

23. *Ibid.* no. 2, which is identical with Aharan Halevi Goldman, *Responsa Divrei Aharon*, Jerusalem, 1981, Y. D. no. 40.

24. Goldman, *op. cit.* no. 35.

25. *Shulchan Aruch, Yoreh Deah* 268:2, *Sifte Kohen*, paragraph 3, based on b. *Yevamot* 47a.

26. Goldman, *op. cit.* no. 35.

27. See S. Zvulun Lieberman, "A Sephardic Ban on Converts", *Tradition* 23 (2), Winter 1988, pp. 22-25. The last proclamation entitled "Reaffirming Our Tradition" was signed by the rabbis and presidents of the congregations of the Syrian and Near Eastern Jewish Communities of Greater New York and New Jersey at a special convocation convened for this purpose on June 3, 1984.

28. *Responsa Helkat Yaakov*, Jerusalem, 1951, v. 1, Yoreh Deah, no. 13.

29. *Ibid.* no. 14. See J. David Bleich, *Contemporary Halakhic* Problems vol. 1, pp. 282-283.

30. David Ellenson, *Tradition in Transition*, Lanham, New York, London, 1989, pp. 92-93.

31. *Ibid.*, chapters 1-8; David Ellenson, *Rabbi Esriel Hildesheimer and the Creation of a Modern Jewish Orthodoxy*, Tuscaloos and London, 1990.

32. Maimonides, *supra* note 1, responsum no. 211.

33. I. Herzog, *Responsa Heikhal Yitzhak*, Tel Aviv, 1960, v. 1, Even Haezer, no. 20, sect. 1, pp. 104-105.

34. *Ibid.* section 2, p. 106.

35. Herzog, *op. cit.* no. 21, pp. 108-109.

36. *Ibid.*, section 2, p. 109: Herzog repeats his anxiety about the validity of conversions in his day in a manner very similar to the other two responsa (supra notes 29 and 34):

> "You should know that even though the law from the time of the *Mishnaic* sages is that *post factum*, they are all converts (even if they did not accept the commandments), I have a very serious suspicion regarding the situation today. In the past in Israel, the violator of Jewish Law was despised and persecuted by his people, therefore when a gentile came to accept Judaism, even though the primary reason that motivated him was for the sake of marriage, he knew that his situation would be very difficult in Jewish society, if he did not behave in accordance with the Torah. This is not the case in our day when so many are free (*hofshim* = secular); not only do they not have any difficulty because of this, but they stand at the head of our people and communities. Therefore, we should be suspicious whether they really accept the *mitzvot*, or whether for some reason, they promise with their mouth but not with their heart."

37. *Responsa Seridei Esh*, Jerusalem, 1977 v. 3, no. 50.

38. *Responsa Mishpatei Uziel*, Tel Aviv, 1935, v. 1, Yoreh Deah, no. 14.

39. *Responsa Eliyahu Guttmacher (Aderet Eliyahu)*, Jerusalem, 1984 Yoreh Deah no. 87.

40. Maimonides, *supra* note 1.

WITHOUT MILAH AND TEVILAH

Richard Rosenthal

In 1892 the C.C.A.R. decided to accept proselytes "without any initiatory rite, ceremony or observance whatever." This significant decision by the Conference came after several years of extensive debate. Isaac M. Wise had first raised the issue in the Philadelphia Conference of 1869; it was discussed at the Pittsburgh Conference in 1885; there were also two separate public discussions of the issue, one raised by Moritz Spitz in 1878 and by Henry Berkowitz in 1890. In this paper, I will look at this process of decision making as an examination of the making of liberal *halakhah*.

Reform Jewish practice has followed the 1892 decision for almost a hundred years. For many of us, perhaps still the majority, it remains as the rule by which we bring people into Judaism. The decision is a fascinating one from several different perspectives. Why did it take several decades to make the decision when the rabbis could set aside all of *kashrut* with a subordinate clause in the Pittsburgh Platform? Yet, conversion is a unique process: one who is not Jewish is brought into the community. The rabbi acts as gatekeeper. It is a very serious role. It changes the status of the person. The Jewish community is larger than the Reform movement; how could the movement act for the entire Jewish community? The process of conversion must raise and attempt to answer questions about Jewish identity and community: What are we, what is essential belief, what is adequate and sincere adherence to Judaism? The question of conversion is by its very nature a *halakhic* question because those who receive the convert must become, even against their will, a *bet din* who must say yes or no to the person who seeks admittance.

Mary Douglas, in *Natural Symbols*, provides us with a useful set of concepts that allow us to understand the changes that occurred in the development of Reform practice and to interpret them. She observes that there is a relationship of the symbols of the human body to the social body. The human body provides us with a set of symbols based on bodily process; social symbols get their meaning from communities with a shared history. The development of Reform Judaism in the nineteenth century was a revolt against the symbol system of Judaism in its earliest, often incoherent, stage. Like most such revolts it often reduced itself to a protest against symbolization as such.[1]

There are three phases in the movement from ritualism. "First, there is the contempt of external ritual forms; second, there is the private internalizing of religious experience; third, there is the movement to humanist philanthropy."[2] "The social body constrains the way the physical body is perceived. The physical experience of the body, always modified by the social categories through which it is known, sustains a particular view of society."[3] These changes are most clearly reflected in the language by which religions speak; it becomes more abstract; the cosmos it describes is more benign; the categories it uses are more undifferentiated. It is the internalization of a new vision of the social body.

Social changes had a devastating effect on the traditional *halakhic* system which depends so heavily on differentiation. Jews have always needed to say *hamavdil*. *Halakhah* defined and limited the body of Israel by limiting the physical body. Medieval *Ashkenazic* Jews, especially, developed a system of personal piety which built walls around Jews in western Christianity. For example, no one has defined the social body more distinctly by the physical body and vice versa than the *Hasidei Ashkenaz*. If we read the bodylanguage in the *Rokeach* we see an obsession with borders, with touching, with body fluids, with a great need for purity at the edge. The most intimate of human connections were governed by *hilkhot niddah*; Jews and Christians were defined in *hilkhot avodah zarah* with its subdivisions of *yayin nesekh* and *stam yenom*, all are physical matters which deal with touching and tasting. *Kashrut* governed bodily intake, *Shabbat* focused on the use of the body in space. The focus was constantly on the body of each Jew and its borders; it assured that all Jews were a single body.

Conversion in Judaism is physical and demands *milah* and *tevilah*. Maimonides restated the tradition beautifully (the laws of *gerut* are codified beginning in *Isurei Biah* 13:1, their presence in that section indicates their physical nature): "Israel entered the covenant through three things: *milah*, *tevilah* and offerings." He continued that whenever an "idolater desires to enter the covenant and to seek shelter under the wings of the *Shekhinah* and receive the yoke of the Torah," he must do the same. The experience of the body of Israel becomes the experience of the bodies of all those who wish to enter the body of Israel.

Conversion by its very nature also raises for us as liberal Jews the issue of pluralism in *halakhah*. Pluralism means that we are serious when we say that differences are legitimate and that we accept the obligation to speak to several distinct audiences at once. What we say must be addressed not only to members of our own movement, but also to all other Jews, religious and secular, and to all persons. The matters with which we deal must be correctly presented in an intellectually acceptable way. Our *halakhah* must speak in a responsible language in a pluralistic society.

The Philadelphia Conference was the first American Reform Conference. David Einhorn and Samuel Adler, who had attended the European Conferences, summoned their colleagues. Like the great *posqim* of the past, they assumed authority to restate the Torah. As one reads Maimonides' introductions, especially to *Mishneh Torah*, one comes away with respect for the power of the *posqim* to act independently. It confirmed the power of the learned elite. It was this power which these early Reform leaders assumed. But even more, they saw themselves as the leaders of the people in a new age. Like Moses they were on their way in the desert at the border of a new Promised Land.

They saw themselves both as *posqim* and prophets. In a new age they assumed the authority which allowed them to make the most radical statements. Individuals, such as Samuel Holdheim and Abraham Geiger, had written more radical proposals. But no body of rabbis had actually voted on them. It was radical German Reform which would come into existence here in America. Not for them was the compromise and misdirection of Isaac M. Wise and the reverends who led communities. They would wrest control from them.

These were German rabbis in America. When they issued their call for the meeting, they invited "theologisch-gebildete Kollegen." They did not want Yeshiva graduates and the self-educated. They wanted men of the university; their ideal was "Bildung"-cultivated men reflecting the cultural ideal of the enlightenment. Their ideal can be described in the same way as Karl Barth spoke of Schleiermacher:"...the fact that Schleiermacher was a theologian did not hinder him in the slightest from also wanting, seeking, effecting, all the things that wisely understood, were best in what the non-theological world of his time was wanting, seeking and effecting...precisely because he was a theologian...he felt himself compelled to be a modern man with all his heart, with all his feelings and with all his strength."[4]

I. M. Wise came to this Conference even though it had been called to oppose him. The Conference agenda had been set by David Einhorn. After passing on a series of general statements expressing a universalist messianic hope, rejecting the distinctions between priest and non-priests, affirming the mission of Israel, negating the belief in resurrection, saying one can pray in any language, the Conference turned to reform of marriage and divorce. Wise's contribution came when they turned to a resolution on circumcision: "The male child of a Jewish mother is no less than the female child - in accordance with a never-disputed principle of Judaism - to be considered a Jew by descent even though uncircumcised."[5] Wise proposed to add the following: "The Abrahamitic circumcision is not a requirement for the entrance into Judaism, and just as its absence does not exclude an Israelite from the Jewish community, so circumcision of proselytes should not be required as an act of initiation." Einhorn opposed this statement revealing a theology in the tradition of Judah HaLevi and the Maharal of Prague. Circumcision serves as a wall to keep impure elements out of Judaism.[6] Wise saw it in the opposite way, the demand for circumcision keeps the best people out. The conference rejected Wise's proposal.

Another public discussion of the issue occurred when Rabbi Moritz Spitz, then rabbi of Emanuel Congregation in Milwaukee, addressed a question to a number of rabbis in 1878.[7] A young man, son of Christian parents, had come to him. He was in love with a Jewish woman, daughter of Orthodox parents. He had proclaimed himself ready to accept Judaism fully, but would not allow himself to be circumcised. After several attempts to separate the couple, her parents had reconciled themselves to allow the marriage if the young man converted even without *milah* (if that were permitted); they wanted to keep their daughter and her descendants Jewish. Rabbi Spitz asked three questions:

> 1. Can he accept the man without *milah*?
> 2. Can he become a full member of a Jewish congregation?
> 3. Does he as a rabbi have the right to marry them?

He knew that from the point of view of *halakhah* there could be no conversion without *milah* and *tevilah*; but it seemed to him that grounds for a different answer exist. Perhaps this situation had already been discussed?

Although he asked in German, this was an American question for it implied that despite the fact that *halakhah* is fixed, in the new world all is possible and perhaps here an exception had already been made. It is not at all clear what answer the rabbi sought from his respondents. But it is clear that he took it for granted that in this new Jewish world nothing was impossible. Law may be set aside; traditions altered and transformed. In 1890, Rabbi Spitz recollected: "...we in our desire to stand justified before the old parents of the Jewish girl wished by an expression of opinion from our colleagues to fortify our position in not admitting the Gentile without the required rite...we refused to admit the gentleman and whether or not the young couple has married each other, we cannot tell.[8]

Bernard Felsenthal answered the question with a monograph on the Jewish attitude toward proselytes. In passing, it is interesting to note that one reason for his answer was to encourage the creation of responsa. The answer to Rabbi Spitz's question, he suggested, depended on the answer to a prior question: Does Judaism want to receive proselytes? Is Judaism a universal religion wanting to share its truth? To show that Judaism has welcomed proselytes, he reviewed the history of *gerut* through Bible, *Talmud* and rabbinic writings. He continued to his own time by quoting Abraham Geiger's response to the *milat gerim* debate of the Philadelphia Conference: "It is a matter of opening wide the halls of Judaism to the enlightened holders of a belief in the pure God concept...."

He continued saying that *milah* was not necessary and suggested a possible new way to receive proselytes. But he did not stop there. He gave us a model of responsible pluralism: A dialogue between himself (as a reformer) with a traditionalist. His conclusion: Conversion without *milah* is theoretically correct; nevertheless do not do it on your own.

The Pittsburgh Platform more than any other document of our Reform past causes a dilemma for us. We read it today with a deep sense of irony; we cannot speak of its positive optimism without putting it in quotation marks. Its total rejection of Jewish national consciousness is a scandal to us, and we normally speak of it only within an apologetic framework. On the other hand, it contains the ideas that we describe as normative in Reform: Acceptance of the science and knowledge of the modern world, the acceptance of all human experience, the insistence on understanding the Jewish experience as a part of the human story. It came, as Michael Meyer has described it[9], at a moment of challenge for Reform. On one side was Felix Adler and Ethical Culture offering a religion for the new age, an ethical faith for a common humanity, and on the other was a newly energized Conservative Judaism which accepted the premise of Reform, but refused to leave the anchor of law. Kaufman Kohler, as Einhorn's heir and successor in New York, had to respond to both Adler and Alexander Kohut, the newly arrived champion of a more traditional approach to Judaism.

It was the Pittsburgh Platform which made Reform Judaism a separate movement. After Pittsburgh, it was no longer possible to minimize the matters that separated the reformers and the conservatives. This represented the intellectual and practical achievement of Kohler. It also marked a reconciliation between Kohler and Wise. The sharp antagonism between East and West was lessened as Kohler's platform came to define Reform. The Philadelphia Conference had used the German language; in Pittsburgh they spoke English. It did not look back at German *Bildung* as the ideal; it spoke in the language of American religious liberalism.[10] In that way, it was a victory for Wise's point of view although he accepted it with reservations.

Our particular issue, *milat gerim*, was discussed at the Conference. In Kohler's opening address to the Conference, he said that the regulation of admission of converts needed to be changed. Echoing Geiger's letter to Zunz, he declared "...to have a grown man who from conviction has with all his heart and soul become a Jew, in order to be admitted, undergo the act of circumcision, is a barbarous cruelty which disfigures and disgraces our ancestral heirloom and our holy mission as priests among mankind. The rite is a national remnant of savage African life, and has no bearing upon the religion preached by Isaiah, Jeremiah and the great Deuteronomic law-giver. It certainly has no sacramental character." [11] He went on to appeal to common sense over "the fanciful and twisted syllogisms of *Talmudic* Law."

Immediately after adopting the platform, the rabbis turned to Kohler's proposal: "We hereby declare that anyone who joins our faith and accepts for himself and children the mission of the Jewish people to live and work for the pure belief in the Only One God and the idea of man as the son of God, is to be accepted as Jew, whether he submits to the Mosaic-rabbinical ordinance or not." [12] In the discussion which followed, Isaac M. Wise objected to the lack of clarity in the resolution, "there must be some form of admission." No one was opposed to Kohler's proposal, but some felt that people in the congregations were not ready for such a radical step. In the end, the discussion closed with the passage of a resolution to appoint a committee to formulate a report to be submitted to the next Conference.

This discussion leaves us with the feeling that the rabbis' were ready to abandon *milah* but did not quite have the courage to proceed. Thus, they decided to wait.

The next Rabbinic Conference following Pittsburgh was the organization of the Central Conference of American Rabbis in 1889. It saw itself in its founding resolution as the continuation of all modern Rabbinical Conferences from the Braunschweig Conference of 1844 onward. This was stated as part of the constitution the C.C.A.R. adopted in Cleveland at its first Conference in 1890. Nevertheless, the Conference never committed itself to these earlier decisions; it only ordered them printed in the *Yearbook*.

Milat gerim was on the agenda of the second convention of the C.C.A.R. Two papers were read and the Conference also received all the materials Henry Berkowitz, then rabbi in Kansas City, had gathered in answer to a letter he had addressed to American rabbis in 1890 which inquired about the necessity of circumcision. Almost all the responses favored the abolition of circumcision, although a number of them cautioned waiting for the right moment. Others felt that it could only be when the rabbis acted in concert. Bernhard Felsenthal again showed an attitude that anticipated pluralism. He repeated his previously published favorable opinion, but continued with a long angry discussion on rabbinic authority, the burden of which stated that rabbis could not speak in the name of the Jewish community. The strongest opponent of the abolition was Moses Mielziner. The tone of these responses made it clear that the writers expected that a day would come when it was no longer required.

The two papers read at the Conference differed on the issue. Aaron Hahn was in favor and Isaac Schwab was opposed. Both of them seemed to have organized their papers by using the material put together in the Felsenthal study.

The question came before the third convention in 1892. I. M. Wise, as chairman of committee on the Initiatory Rites of Proselytes, gave his report. In it he reviewed the material from the previous year and then presented a study to prove that *milah* and *tevilah* had no basis in *Tanakh* and *Mishnah*, and that the *Tanaim* had a difference of opinion over what was required of *gerim*. In any case, because of this indecision, the rites are only custom and not law and may be abolished. Kaufman Kohler challenged him, not on the abolition of the rite, but on his scholarship. Kohler was to have the final voice after a bitter debate. The resolution as rewritten by Kohler finally passed twenty-five ayes to five nays. Four of the nays wrote brief statements which explained their vote against the resolution: They were afraid, in the words of Maurice H. Harris, that "the admission of proselytes without *milah* (sic) is the entering wedge for the abolition of this rite altogether."[13] The vote probably did not reflect the true opinion of the Conference. A few older members held back, younger members, recent Hebrew Union College graduates must have been in favor; the majority of the members of the CCAR were not in attendance at the convention. The resolution was certainly never questioned again.

What can we conclude from this? (1) The character of the Reform movement was shaped by this debate. Moshe Davis called it the "point of no return" separating the Reformers from the Historical School.[14] Reform Jews were certainly distinct from the newly arriving Eastern European Jews and their rabbinic leaders (to whom this entire debate must have seemed like nonsense). Ethical culture and Unitarians saw in the platform a break with universalism and an insistence on Jewish uniqueness. (2) No great multitudes awaited enlightenment, but it made conversion for the sake of marriage easier and realistically possible. (3) It is interesting to note that only one of the discussants in the large amount of material published in the Central Conference of American Rabbis *Yearbook* of 1891 actually mentioned pain. Adolph Moses[15] wrote: "The pain is excruciating, the wound takes between four and five weeks to heal." Jewish tradition took this difficulty in consideration by postponing immersion until after the convert had healed from the circumcision. In fact, the Rambam states that one should not immerse before circumcision because he might find the circumcision too difficult and the immersion would have made him Jewish already.[16] (4) By relinquishing control of the body, the nature of the body of Israel was dramatically redefined. Israel was seen as humanity; conversion an affirmation of the human. There should be no barriers between Jews and Christian (in his address at the Pittsburgh Conference, Kaufman Kohler said "Christian" when he is referring to non-Jews). No one addressed the question why anyone would want to be Jewish when it adds nothing and was only a confirmation of the human.

It may be better to read all this with the sense of irony that Reinhold Niebuhr has taught us as we look at all expressions of American messianic hopes. The Jewish hope is the universal hope, the Jew is every man. But Jews keep on being Jews and the world remains the world. As H. Richard Niebuhr has written of Protestant liberalism: "...the idea of the coming kingdom was robbed of its dialectical element. It was all fulfillment of promise without judgment. It was thought to be growing out of the present so that no great crisis needed to intervene between the order of grace and order of glory. In its one-sided view of progress...this liberalism was indeed naively optimistic."[17]

Notes

1. Mary Douglas, *Natural Symbols*, introduction to the New Edition, pp. xix ff.

2. Mary Douglas, *Ibid.*, p. 7.

3. Mary Douglas, *Ibid.*, p. 65.

4. Karl Barth, *From Rousseau to Ritschl*, London, 1959, p. 315.

5. *Protokolle...*,p. 10. The translation is from Central Conference of American Rabbis Yearbook 1891, p. 120.

6. Einhorn's Prayer Book *Olat Tamid* contains a ritual statement of belief for proselytes; the only prayer book to do so.

7. His question is printed in B. Felsenthal, *Zur Proselytenfrage im Judenthum*, Chicago 1878, pp. 7ff.

8. Moritz Spitz in *Jewish Voice*, Oct. 17, 1890 quoted in Central Conference of American Rabbis Yearbook 1892, p. 123.

9. Michael A Meyer, *Response to Modernity*, New York, Oxford 1988, pp. 265ff.

10. William Hutchinson characterizes Protestant modernism by three things: adaptation of religious ideas to modern culture, God immanent in human development and revealed through it, and progression to the realization of the Kingdom of God; *The Modernist Impulse in American Protestantism*, Oxford 1976, p. 2. This is a perfect description of the Pittsburgh Platform.

11. *Authentic Report of the Proceedings of the Rabbinical Conference held at Pittsburgh*, Nov. 16, 17, 18, 1885 reprinted in Walter Jacob (ed.) *The Changing World of Reform Judaism*, Pittsburgh, 1985, p. 101.

12. *Ibid.*, pp. 111f.

13. Central Conference of American Rabbis Yearbook 1892, p. 38.

14. Moshe Davis, *The Emergence of Conservative Judaism*, Philadelphia 1963, p. 201.

15. He had studied medicine, see *Jewish Encyclopedia*.

16. *Turei Zahav* to *Yoreh Deah* 268:2.

17. H. Richard Niebuhr, *The Kingdom of God in America*, Chicago, New York, 1937, p. 193.

CONVERSION IN REFORM *HALAKHAH*

Walter Jacob

The question of *gerut* and matters related to it have been peripheral to Judaism during most of the last fifteen hundred years. The early history has been the subject of many studies.[1] Although there was considerable *Talmudic* discussion as well as a minor tractate on the subject, it became less important after the Council of Nicaea which prohibited conversion to Judaism in Christian lands, and somewhat later in other countries. It was dangerous to seek converts. The issue of conversion to Judaism became theoretical, although a small number of individuals joined us through the ages. They were conspicuous and have often been recorded for that reason. The great codes of Alfasi, Maimonides, Caro, and others who wrote earlier, only dealt with the subject in a brief summary fashion.

Conversion has become important again since the Emancipation, although our first concern was conversion from Judaism to Christianity. In this period, conversion to Judaism once more became possible without incurring religious or civil penalty. Some initial discussion was stirred by the Napoleonic Sanhedrin (1806) in which the French government asked the Jewish community about the status of marriages between Jews and non-Jews. Although this question did not deal with conversion, it meant that the issue of family status was given new significance. The Sanhedrin provided an answer which dealt with the question in a satisfactory manner both from the French and Jewish point of view.

It stated that such marriages were considered binding civilly. They could not be invested with religious meaning, but they should also not evoke a *herem* (ban). This entire matter, of course, was difficult for the Assembly.[2] The discussions on similar issues which followed did not deal with the question of *gerut* as that might have been dangerous. It was not to become important until the second portion of the century when it was the subject of debate at various rabbinic conferences and synods. There were some discussions of conversion and the methods appropriate for it in Jewish periodicals,[3] but this paper will look in that direction. When the issue surfaced at rabbinic meetings, we will find the debate raging over the ritual rather than the substance of conversion.

This paper is divided into two segments; the first will summarize the Reform position as expressed through synods, conferences, and responsa. The second section will analyze these developments and seek the rationale behind them.

European Rabbinic Conference

At the meeting in Braunschweig (1846), the assembled delegates dealt with the subject of mixed marriage. They gave religious recognition to mixed marriages and thus, went further than the Sanhedrin of Napoleon. However, this was done inadvertently as they had not remembered the Sanhedrin's statement accurately and merely sought to reiterate it. Those who had voted for change did so under the assumption that the state would permit all children of such a marriage to be raised as Jews.[4]

At the rabbinic convention which met in Frankfurt in July of 1845, a great many issues were discussed, but mixed marriage and conversion were not among them. The convention held in Breslau in July of 1846 also largely turned to other matters, however, the radical Holdheim suggested that rabbis officiate at the marriage of Jews and non-Jews.[5] In Leipzig in 1869, a number of questions which dealt with offsprings of mixed marriage were introduced. The main item on the agenda was the question whether an uncircumcised boy of a Jewish mother could be considered as Jewish; this was decided positively and traditional sources were cited. The first longer discussion in the matter of status therefore dealt with a single ritual issue rather than a broader philosophical approach. In the same rabbinical convention it was suggested that the resolution of Braunschweig, which stated that marriage between Jews and non-Jews was not prohibited, be accepted but no action was taken on that motion.

The Synod of Augsburg in 1871 again dealt with the status of a child, born of a Jewish mother, who had not been circumcised. For the first time the subject of conversion for the sake of marriage was discussed in light of the *Talmudic* law which prohibited such a conversion. The meeting decided that those who converted from Christianity were not subject to any *Talmudic* stricture, as Christians were monotheists not idolators.[6] The broader consequences of this decision were not debated.

American Rabbinic Conference

The meeting of Philadelphia held in 1869 was the first major rabbinic conference held in the United States, dealt with the status of an uncircumcised child of a Jewish mother, and declared the child to be Jewish in every respect[7]. The Reform leader, David Einhorn, put it in the following way: "Circumcision belongs, indeed, to the most important Jewish obligations, but the uncircumcised of Jewish origin was as much a member of the Jewish community as anyone who elects to practice any other commandment whose omission involves the punishment of expulsion." This statement dealt with all Jews, not converts alone, and we should remember that there was a movement among the more radical reformers in Germany to eliminate circumcision.[8]

The delegates to the Pittsburgh meeting of 1885 felt that this question of circumcision for converts needed further investigation and appointed a committee of five to deal with it in an appropriate fashion. No resolution was passed at that conference although those in attendance seemed inclined toward not requiring it.

The entire matter of circumcision for proselytes was discussed in detail at the second meeting of the Central Conference of American Rabbis held in 1891, in Baltimore. A lengthy report was provided by Rabbi Aaron Hahn. He demonstrated that in the past *milah* had been a consistent requirement but he favored its abolition. A colleague, Rabbi Isaac Schwab, supported the opposite view and pointed out that this ritual had always been part of Judaism; it should be continued. Any change should not be made under the guise of rabbinic precedent as there was none. He favored continuing this discussion and widened it to include everything connected with the admission of proselytes. As converts to Judaism were small in number; this was not a pressing issue.

Earlier in 1890, Rabbi Henry Berkowitz of Philadelphia had sent a circular letter which posed the question of circumcision for converts to many colleagues, both Reform and traditional, soliciting their written response. It is interesting that this ritual rather than the process of conversion or the desirability of converts or any other issue connected with conversion was discussed at such length.

This seemed to have been a dramatic issue which aroused strong emotions and many felt compelled to respond. Let us see how they responded. Isaac Mayer Wise reaffirmed an earlier stance expressed in *The American Israelite*. He rejected the need for circumcision for proselytes, yet he stated that this was only a theoretical position. In practice he realized that remaining uncircumcised would make the life of the proselyte difficult and so he favored the rite for the sake of Jewish unity. Bernard Felsenthal agreed with Wise's conclusion, but utilized a different line of reasoning. He indicated both in his response, and in an earlier long article[9] that he opposed *milah* as a requirement for proselytes unless it was done for the sake of the larger Jewish community. He felt that a rabbi could appropriately admit a convert, without circumcision, to his own congregation, but could not expect that individual to be looked upon as a Jew by others in the Jewish community.[10]

Professor Moses Mielziner felt that this matter needed to be decided by a rabbinic body not by individuals, as otherwise it would lead to chaos within the Jewish community. He personally felt that circumcision was required, otherwise it might also lapse as a ritual for Jewish children born to Jewish parents.

Rabbi Emmanuel Schreiber looked at the entire question from a modern historical perspective and mentioned the Reform Society of Frankfurt which had eliminated the requirements for circumcision altogether for Jews in 1842. This had elicited a very strong negative reaction. Some forty-one rabbis wrote in opposition; others stated that although such a child would be considered as a Jew, it should not be permitted to participate in congregational life until circumcised. In the final analysis, Schreiber left it to the convert himself to decide upon circumcision.

Rabbi Max Landsberg indicated that circumcision should be eliminated for proselytes; Rabbi Gottheil felt *milah* was a barrier which should be removed as did Rabbi A. Moses, while Rabbi S. Hecht felt that such a change should be made only after the most careful deliberation.

Rabbi Kaufmann Kohler did not respond directly to the question but simply defended the ritual of circumcision as a religious symbolic rite; he had dealt with this matter earlier in Pittsburgh. Rabbi M. Samfield replied with a lengthy statement in which he advocated the elimination of circumcision while Rabbi Spitz felt that circumcision was essential.

The Orthodox rabbi of New Orleans, Henry Illoway, considered it along with *Shabbat* as a main element of Judaism. It was therefore an absolute requirement. Rabbi Emil G. Hirsch, the radical reformer, traced the matter historically and concluded that the rite had no meaning for us in his century.

We should note that more basic issues were not discussed at all by any of these leaders. The matter was not resolved until the third rabbinic conference held in New York in 1892. A resolution offered by Isaac Mayer Wise stated that a rabbi along with two associates could admit a convert without any accompanying ritual; this was adopted by a vote of twenty-five to five[11] At the discussion immediately following, it was suggested that some statistics on conversion be kept and it was so ordered,[12] but this was never carried out.

Within the same *Yearbook* a statement by Samuel Hirsch, who could not be present a year earlier, was read into the record. It also opposed the requirement of circumcision. The committee then expanded the discussion to include *tevilah* and continued with a long discussion of both matters in the rabbinic literature. The arguments were primarily concerned with a refutation of Schwab's analysis of the rabbinic texts; he had favored retention of the requirement.

The committee concluded that no initiatory rites were Biblical. Later, after they had been established, they became "customary" but not absolutely required.

This lengthy debate over circumcision for those born as Jews and of converts which stretched over a period of almost fifty years may seem strange. However, we should see it as a boundary issue through which Reform was to define itself. Other matters like the language of prayer, specific prayers, the second day of *Yom Tov*, etc., had a long developmental history. They had been added to Judaism and could be deleted. Circumcision, which began in the days of Abraham, was an ultimate boundary issue. Furthermore, as circumcision had been turned into an issue by Paul, it was also a line of demarcation between Judaism and Christianity. Here was a debate over the basic direction which the movement would take.

American Reform Responsa

As we look at the later *halakhic* discussion of conversion and requirement for it, we will find that most of this has taken place through the responsa literature developed by the Responsa Committee of the Central Conference as well as the responsa written independently by Solomon B. Freehof and myself. These *halakhic* discussions have taken two forms. There is a large body of formal responsa as well as *halakhic* correspondence. As we analyze the subjects of these responsa, and we should remember that responsa by their very nature deal with specific questions or with unusual circumstances. One hundred and sixty-six responsa and *halakhic* letters have dealt with *gerut* or matters related to it. This is less than ten percent of a total of one thousand and ten responsa and an equal number of halakhic letters.[13]

The following subjects have been treated: adult status, including patrilineal descent: 36; children of a mixed marriage, their status or nature of their conversion: 43; education toward conversion: 12; relationship of a convert to her/his non-Jewish family, particularly in connection of funeral arrangement, burial, etc: 12; circumcision: 12; perspective convert or unconverted member of family participation on synagogue or home rituals:7; Orthodox objections to Reform Conversion: 5; *miqvaot*: 5; name to be selected by the convert: 5; non-Jew as member of congregation: 5; apostate convert: 2; status of Unitarians/Ethical Culture: 2; *Aliyah*: 1; cantor or lay officiation and conversion: 3. The rest were miscellaneous issues and inquiries.

Among the early responsa was a question on the conversion of children in a mixed marriage. Kaufmann Kohler (1919) made it quite clear that a rabbi should not conduct mixed marriages, yet a child of such a mixed marriage may be raised as a Jew and converted through Jewish education. He urged that the rabbi attempt to convince the mother to become Jewish for the sake of a Jewish home.[14]

The paucity of responsa on this subject in the first four decades of this century indicate that conversion played a minor role in Jewish life until the 1950's. The nature of the discussion gradually shifted from the narrow traditional focus upon ritual to an acceptance of converts with as few obstacles as possible. Conversion for the sake of marriage was accepted in contrast to the tradition.[15] There was a clear acknowledgement that instruction was primary; and that became the policy through the "Report on Mixed Marriage and Intermarriage".

Interestingly, Solomon B. Freehof did not include conversion in the first volume of *Reform Jewish Practice* published in 1944, but only in the second published in 1952 in a chapter entitled "Marriage and Conversion." Actually only one section dealt with the conversion of children and restated the conclusion of the 1947 report.[16]

The requirements of conversion and the theological issues involved were avoided, though Solomon B. Freehof dealt with conversion in a more general way (1963) when asked about converting a theological student. He discussed the old question whether conversion is a *mitzvah*. It is not listed among the six hundred and thirteen commandments, nor do we consider it necessary for any person's salvation, so we may properly hesitate about accepting a prospective convert.[17]

In recent years a desire for a clearer statement of standards has become evident.[18] The need for a formal course of *gerut* with a specific curriculum arose.[19] The Union of American Hebrew Congregations' Commission on Outreach published such manuals in the 1980s.

We can see from formal responsa and the *halakhic* correspondence that every effort to be inclusive was made. A child, who according to the 1947 document cited above might not be considered Jewish until Confirmation, would actually be considered Jewish upon enrollment in the Religious School; in other words, the intent of a Jewish education was sufficient.[20] Similarly an effort was made to permit conversion through cantors or lay people in isolated communities where conversion would otherwise be difficult.[21] This was not the preferred way, but *b'diavad* it was acceptable and *l'hat-hilah* possible.

It, of course, became necessary to fight against Orthodox aspersions,[22] but this never became the subject of a formal responsum.

In the period of heavy Russian Jewish immigration from 1980 onward, numerous questions about the Jewish status of the immigrants arose. We again did our best to be inclusive and to welcome these individuals who had suffered persecution even when their status was uncertain.[23] As individuals from ethnic communities considered conversion, a variety of special questions were raised.[24]

It is interesting to note that after a long period of questions which dealt primarily with more theoretical matters and status, ritual questions again became significant in the 1980's, so questions about the use of a *miqveh* and the ritual of immersion were raised for the first time in this century.[25] Some have expressed desire to create a public conversion ceremony and the positive and negative aspects of this were discussed.[26]

Conclusions

As we have read a summary of debates as well as some of the responsa, we must ask what was and is the justification for the changes which have been made. They are radical and represent a new view of conversion. Yet the Reform movement views them as strongly rooted in the past.

Let us begin with the debate on circumcision. There is, of course, no problem about the uncircumcised child of a Jewish mother. As long as the mother is Jewish, according to tradition, the child is Jewish whether circumcised or not. The obligation for the *b'rit* rests first on the father, then on the mother and finally a *bet din* may supervise the circumcision. When the child reaches maturity, the obligation then is his. The lack of circumcision would be considered a sin but did not disqualified that individual in any way as a Jew. In that debate the Reformers were completely in agreement with their more traditional counterparts.

However, when we turned to the matter of circumcision for proselytes, we see a division in the ranks of the Reform leaders which reflected the mood of the period. Some individuals felt that the rituals of Judaism were no longer significant. The intellectual content was of primary importance and the rituals represented an educational tool of a previous age.[27] This theoretical stand was used particularly with rituals of the rabbinic period, however, circumcision is Biblical and was mentioned in connection with Abraham and others.[28] It was therefore more difficult to eliminate circumcision for proselytes than some other rituals. In addition, some rabbis refused to consider its elimination for the sake of the unity of the Jewish people. A number of rabbis also felt that such an important decision should not be undertaken by individuals but only by all Reform rabbis together so that standards for conversion would be uniform.

All rested their case on the principle stated in the *Pittsburgh Platform*: "We recognize in the Mosaic legislation a system of training the Jewish people for its mission during its national life in Palestine, and today we accept as binding only the moral laws and maintain only such ceremonies as elevate and sanctify our lives, but reject all such as are not adapted to the views and habits of modern civilization." Although much tradition has returned to Reform Judaism, circumcision and *hatafat dam* have not been uniformly required of perspective converts to this day, and we have more or less accepted the resolution passed by the third rabbinic conference of 1892, which stated that no accompanying ritual was required for converts.

Equally radical has been the acceptance of individuals for conversion who intend to marry a Jew. The tradition long ago decided to reject any convert who sought gain from the conversion whether it was economic advantage or family status.[29] That decision followed considerable debate in the first century between the followers of Hillel and Shamai. Presumably the decision not to accept such converts reflected contemporary social conditions.

How can we justify the Reform change? We have done so by stating that our current social conditions differ from those in the first century. We are not dealing with a pagan environment and those who come to us are already monotheists, usually Christians whose bond to their religion has become weakened or perhaps has vanished all together. When they marry a Jew, they are converting for the sake of family unity; the advantage is ours, not theirs, as conversion will assure that the children are raised as Jews. We, therefore, following the *halakhic* tendency which permits change in the face of new social and political conditions. What was perceived as a danger in earlier times may now be an opportunity. We have reopened a debate which took place in the first century and have come to a different conclusion for us in the late twentieth century. We should note that some of our Orthodox colleagues have followed the same path and found a variety of rationales for doing so, particularly in the lands of Western Europe in the early part of this century.[30]

We have made other changes which represent accommodations to our time as well. The traditional texts and the codes of Joseph Karo and Moses Maimonides required a prospective convert to be introduced to some major and some minor *mitzvot*. Nothing more detailed was specified. We have developed this into a thorough introduction to Judaism and placed our emphasis upon the intellectual understanding of Judaism as well as acquaintance with its rituals. The prospective convert usually studies all, the major aspects of Judaism, and is introduced to Bible, *Talmud*, the medieval literature, philosophy, history, holidays, life cycle rituals and a good deal else. In this way we have sought to bring a good understanding of Judaism to the prospective converts and enable them to become part of the Jewish community.

Equally radical has been our quiet acceptance of children of mixed marriages through enrollment in Religious School. The ceremonies of *Bar/Bat Mitzvah* or Confirmation established their Jewishness without a formal conversion. This practice followed for decades was made official by the Central Conference in 1947.[31]

There is no basis for this in the tradition and it represented a reaction to mixed marriage. No official conversion at the initial enrollment of the child took place, in an effort to cause as little discomfort to the non Jewish parent as possible. The enrollment in Religious School, which often represented a concession to family peace or to grandparents, slowly evolved into a Jewish commitment. This represented a realistic approach.

The issue of questionable conversion has always been with us and in many periods those who stated that they were Jewish either as converts or returning Marranos were quietly accepted.[32] We have sought to accept both converts from other countries where the precise conditions of conversion are not known to us, as well as more informal conversions which may have taken place in the Soviet Union. Whenever these individuals sought to identify themselves as Jews, we have felt that this was done in good faith, accepted the individuals, and have done our best to encourage them to further study and a greater commitment. Here we have once more followed a lenient path for the sake of the individuals involved.

Although *tevilah* has been part of conversion since the first century and is mentioned by all of the codes, it has played no part in Reform debate until quite recently. It was brought up incidentally at the end of the last century but were no further discussions until the nineteen-eighties. This reflects a lingering doubt about ritual requirements and although those requirements now once more seem more significant, we have only slowly returned to them. As we look over the development of Reform *Halakhah* and the radical changes which have taken place in our conversion procedures and practices, we will see that we began with radical changes and subsequently developed *halakhah* in accordance with specific needs of our age. We have not rejected the past but have modified it in order to deal with current problems, as tradition has always done until the nineteenth century, thereby kept the *halakhah* alive and functioning in our Reform movement.

At various times during the last century, Reform rabbis have asked that we expand our efforts and actively seek converts among the unaffiliated Gentile community which is friendly to Judaism. This impulse to seek converts in the broader community was also part the mandate of the Outreach Commission of the Union of American Hebrew Congregations which was established in the late 1970's. We have, however, not done so. We, along with tradition, have not seen missionizing as one of the six-hundred and thirteen commandments. We have felt a good bit of discomfort with such a notion particularly as we have suffered from attempts to convert us for so many centuries. Although such efforts are now relatively rare in comparison to an earlier age, we have been stopped by the memory of those attempts directed toward us.

As we look back over almost a half century of fairly intensive discussion of converts and conversion, we can begin to draw some conclusions. The basic questions, sometimes already asked in the *Talmud*, have been raised again. In this century we have almost always taken a positive and open attitude with the hope of welcoming converts and integrating them into the community. Every effort has been made to provide positive answers while at the same time drawing clear lines of demarcation between us and the Christian community.

We have redefined what is important in conversion by including the ritual requirements, but leaving them as secondary. Learning and acquiring a practical understanding of Judaism ranks first for us and we have made this clear in our *halakhic* development.

The initial open attitude toward non-Jews, particularly in connection with burial in our cemeteries, was seen as a friendly gesture not as a way of breaking down barriers of distinction between Judaism and Christianity. As that was not always clear in the early responsa, we have tried to be more specific in other areas as they have arisen and made those distinctions quite clear. The entire area of personal and family relationships with non-Jews will always have many gray areas which cannot be defined in advance, but we are now making the attempt to define all that is possible. Patrilineal descent has helped this in some ways and made it more difficult in others. The primary difficulty with that decision has been in its lack of definition of what are appropriate Jewish acts and when they lead to acceptance into the community. We are at an initial stage of working out solutions to these problems for ourselves and for the entire North American Jewish community.

Some efforts to deal with these matters jointly have been made, but thus far without success.[31] At the same time, local efforts to create joint conversion procedures were undertaken in a number of North American communities; the best known was that of Denver, but all have thus far failed.

Notes

1. Bamberger, Bernard J. *Proselytism in the Talmudic Period* Cincinnati, 1939, p. 588; Braude, William G. *Jewish Proselyting in the First Five Centuries of the Common Era: The Age of the Tannaim and Amoraim.* Providence, 1940; Cohen, Shaye J. D. *Josephus in Galilee and Rome: His Vita and Development as a Historian.* Leiden, 1979. "Conversion to Judaism in Historical Perspective: From Biblical Israel to Postbiblical Judaism." CF 36.4 (Summer 1983): 31-45; Geiger, Abraham. *Urschrift und Übersetzungen der Bibel in ihrer Abhängigkeit von der inneren Entwicklung des Judenthums.* Breslau, 1957; Golb, Norman. *Jewish Proselytism - A Phenomenon in the Religious History of Early Medieval Europe,* Cincinnati, 1987; M. Guttmann, *Das Judentum und Seine Umwelt,* Berlin, 1927, p. 602. Juster, Jean *Les Juifs dans l'empire romain.* 2 vols. Paris, 1914; Klausner, *Joseph From Jesus to Paul.* Trans. William F. Stinespring, New York, 1943; Moore, George, F. *Judaism in the First Centuries of the Christian Era: The Age of the Tannaim.* 3 vols. Cambridge, MA 1927-30; Rosenbloom, Joseph R. *Conversion to Judaism: From the Biblical Period to the Present.* Cincinnati, 1978; Schürer Emil, *The History of the Jewish People in the Age of Jesus Christ (175 B.C. - A.D. 135),* ed. Geza Vermes and Fergus Millar. 3 vols. Edinburgh, 1973-86; Stern, Menahem. *Greek and Latin Authors on Jews and Judaism.* 3 vols. Jerusalem, 1974-84; Wacholder, Ben Zion. "Cases of Proselytizing in the Tosafist Responsa." JQR 51; (1960-61): 288-315.

2. M. Diogene, Tama, *Transactions of the Parisian Sanhedrin,* London, 1807.

3. A. Geiger; *Wissenschaftliche Zeitschrift für jüdische Theologie,* Isaac Leeser, *The Occident;* Isaac M. Wise, *The American Israelite.*

4. *Central Conference of American Rabbis Yearbook*, New York, Volume 1 pp 81ff.

5. *Central Conference of American Rabbis Yearbook*, New York, Vol I, p 98.

6. *Central Conference of American Rabbis Yearbook*, New York, Vol I, p 113.

7. *Central Conference of American Rabbis Yearbook*, New York, Vol I, p 120.

8. This was a movement of the Frankfurt Reformfreunde led by Theodor Creizenach who published a call for the abolition of circumcision in 1843 as well as the movement of the *Shabbat* to Sunday; these decisions led to widespread protest by Reform and to change the Orthodox rabbis.

9. *Monatsschrift für die Wissenschaft des Judenthums*, 1878, pp 236-240.

10. *Central Conference of American Rabbis Yearbook*, New York, Vol II, p 94.

11. The paper written by Isaac Mayer Wise indicated that according to his reading of the text it was not required by the *Torah* and in fact that there was no blessing for it recorded before Alfasi in the eleventh century. His interpretation of the *Mishnah* also made no such requirement but left it as an option. He theorized that the *b'rit milah* was a substitute for the *qorban* which was no longer possible. As he looked at this matter historically, he felt that there was no record of *milah* before John Hyrcanus and the forced Edomite conversion to Judaism in the second century B.C.E. Wise proposed admission before a rabbi and two associates. The crucial element would be acceptance of the Israelite covenant. "He resolved that the Central Conference of American Rabbis, assembled this day in this city of New York, considers it lawful and proper for any officiating rabbi, assisted by no less than two associates, to accept into the sacred covenant of Israel and declare fully affiliated to the congregation any honorable and intelligent person, who desires such affiliation, without any initiatory rite, ceremony or observance whatever; provided such person be sufficiently acquainted with the faith, doctrine and canon of Israel; that nothing derogatory to such person's moral and mental character is suspected; that it is his or her free will and choice to embrace the cause of Judaism; and that he or she declare verbally and in a document signed and sealed before such officiating rabbi and his associates his or her intention and firm resolve.

    1. To worship the One, Sole and Eternal God, and none besides him.
    2. To be conscientiously governed in his or her doings and omissions in life by God's laws ordained for the child and image of the Maker and Father of all, the sanctified son or daughter of the divine covenant.
    3. To adhere in life and death, actively and faithfully, to the sacred cause and mission of Israel, as marked out in Holy Writ. Be it furthermore

Resolved, that a committee of three be appointed to report to this conference formulas of the two documents, viz., one to be signed by the proselyte and witnesses, to remain in the hands of the officiating rabbi, and another to be signed by the officiating rabbi and his associates, to be delivered to the proselyte.".

Ibid., III, 73-95.

12. *Cental Conference of American Rabbis Yearbook*, New York, Vol III, p 36.

13. Early responsa by various authors: 72; responsa by Solomon B. Freehof: 433; responsa by Walter Jacob: 505; *halakhic* correspondence of Solomon B. Freehof: 640; *halakhic* correspondence and telephone notes of Walter Jacob: 420.

14. W. Jacob, *American Reform Responsa*, #60. During the same decade, in 1914 and 1919, a number of questions arose about the burial of non-Jewish wives in a Jewish cemetery. The answer given by Kaufmann Kohler indicated that this was permitted as the entire cemetery itself was not considered sacred. Gotthardt Deutsch wrote a similar responsum in 1919 and presented the same conclusion for our Reform congregations but he pointed out that traditional congregations would permit it only in the case of an emergency. He provided thorough rabbinic documentation. A subsequent responsum by Jacob Mann in 1936 dealt with an individual who continued to be a believing Christian and Mann decided that this burial should be prohibited, with one member of the committee, Julius Rappaport, dissenting. The matter was treated again by Solomon B. Freehof in 1963 in a more thorough responsum with many citations.

15. S. B. Freehof - *Correspondence*, 1957.

16. S. B. Freehof, *Reform Jewish Practice, Vol II*, New York, 1952, pp. 85 ff.

17. S. B. Freehof, *Recent Reform Responsa*, Cincinnati, 1963.

18. W. Jacob, *American Reform Responsa*, New York, 1983, #65.

19. W. Jacob, *Questions and Reform Jewish Answers*, New York, #124.

20. S. B. Freehof - *Manuscript Responsa*, 1965.

21. S. B. Freehof, *Manuscript Responsa*, 1972, 1973; S. B. Freehof, *Current Reform Responsa*, Cincinnati, 1969, #25.

22. S. B. Freehof, *Manuscript Responsa*, Cincinnati, 1980.

23. W. Jacob, *Contemporary Reform Responsa*, New York, 1987, #56 - #60, *Questions and Reform Jewish Answers*, New York, 1992, #129 ff.

24. W. Jacob, *Questions and Reform Jewish Answers*, New York, 1992, #1321 ff.

25. W. Jacob, *Contemporary American Reform Responsa*, New York, 1987, #44, #47.

26. W. Jacob, *Contemporary American Reform Responsa*, New York, 1987, #46.

27. W. Jacob (ed.) *The Pittsburgh Platform in Retrospect*, p. 108, Pittsburgh, 1985.

28. Gen 17:10; 21:4; 34:14; Ex 12:48; Lev 12:3, etc.

29. Gerim 1.7; *Yad, Hil. Issurei Biah* 13:14.

30. David Hoffman *Melamed L'Hoil*, New York, 1954, #83.

31. *Central Conference of American Rabbis Yearbook*, 1947.

32. H. J. Zimmels, *Die Marranen in der Rabbinischen Literatur*, Berlin 1932.

31. I have participated in efforts with Orthodox and Conservative representatives to create a common conversion procedure for those contemplating *aliyah*, however, after two years those discussions in New York and Jerusalem failed (1989).

SELECTED REFORM RESPONSA

These responsa are a representative selection on conversion chosen from more than one thousand American Reform responsa published in the twentieth century. We are grateful to the Central Conference of American Rabbis and the Hebrew Union College Press for permission to reproduce them.

CONVERSION WITHOUT FORMAL INSTRUCTION

Walter Jacob

QUESTION: A couple in a mixed marriage have maintained a Jewish life-style for more than a decade. He is Jewish, and she came from a Protestant background. They were married civilly, and she had not practiced her religion or believed its tenets for many years prior to her marriage. She has received no formal instruction in Judaism, but for the last decade she has lived a Jewish life. She has attended services during the *Yamim Noraim*, and intermittently during the year, has participated in many programs of the Temple and its Sisterhood, enrolled in some adult education classes, and raised her children as Jews. The family observes Jewish holidays at home by lighting candles and making *Qiddush* each Friday evening and on the eve of holidays; they erect a *Sukkah* and light *Hanukah* lights. She considers herself Jewish, as do her friends. She would now like to have this "Jewishness" recognized officially. She does not wish to attend the Introduction to Judaism class for young new converts. She would also feel out of place at the standard conversion ceremonies which her congregation conducts publicly. How can she officially be considered as Jewish? (F.L., Miami, FL)*

ANSWER: Let us begin by reviewing the Reform discussion and the development of the tradition. The American Reform discussions of conversion from 1890 onward make it quite clear that the principal requirements were intellectual; we have been more concerned with understanding than ritual ("*Milat Gerim,*" *CCAR Yearbook*, 1947, pp. 15ff; see also #69-71 in Walter Jacob, *American Reform Responsa*). In keeping with this emphasis, Introduction to Judaism classes have been organized by virtually all congregations. In larger communities, some of the congregations have joined together and offered centralized classes on a year-round basis along with individualized instruction by the congregational rabbi. Traditional Judaism, of course, also requires instruction, but usually places the emphasis upon the ritual duties incumbent upon either the man or the woman, rather than on a more general background. For traditional Jews, the ritual of conversion is of primary importance, irrespective of the instruction which had taken place.

The traditional requirements for conversion are clear (*Yev.* 46, 47; *Shulhan Arukh, Yoreh Deah* 268; *Yad Hil. Issurei Biah* 15); a court of three is necessary. Prospective converts must be warned that they are joining a persecuted community, and that many new obligations will be incumbent upon them. They were to bring a sacrifice in the days when the Temple stood, and males had to be circumcised and take a ritual bath. To this day, the requirements of a *Bet Din, Tevilah*, and *Berit* still remain for traditional Jews. The sources are clear on the requirements, but considerable discussion about them exists in the *Talmud*. For example, R. Eliezer stated that if a prospective male convert was either circumcised or took a ritual bath, he was considered a proselyte. R. Joshua insisted on both, and his point of view was adopted (*Yev.* 46b). Hillel and Shammai disagreed about a prospective male convert who was already circumcised: *Bet Shammai* insisted that blood must be drawn from him, while *Bet Hillel* stated that one may simply accept that circumcision without drawing blood (*Shab.* 135a). The Rabbinic authorities decided in favor of *Bet Shammai* (*Shulhan Arukh, Yoreh Deah* 268.1; *Yad, Hil. Issurei Biah* 14.5). There were differences of opinion about steps necessary for the ritual of conversion in ancient times. The *Talmud* also contains a variety of opinions about the desirability of accepting converts. These reflect historic competition with Christianity, persecution, etc., in the early centuries of our era.

The *Talmudic* discussions insist that the convert must join Judaism without any ulterior motives, and if such are present, the conversion is void (*Yev.* 24b). Of course, the opinion applies only prospectively, not retrospectively, and *bediavad* they were accepted.

Some authorities were more lenient in regard to ulterior motives, so Hillel (*Shab.* 31a) readily accepted a convert who stated that he wished eventually to become a high priest. R. Hiya accepted a woman who wanted to marry one of his students (*Men.* 44a). In modern times, although most Orthodox authorities would reject those who seek to join us for the sake of marriage, some would accept them in order to avoid the conversion by Reform rabbis (Mendel Kirshbaum, *Menahem Meshiv*, #9), because civil marriage has preceded, or because the couple is living together (David Hoffman, *Melamed Lehoil, Even Haezer* 8, 10; *Yoreh Deah* 85). Similar arguments have been advance by Meshulam Kutner in *Uketora Yaasu*, and by Moses Feinstein in *Igerot Mosheh, Even Haezer* # 27. However, the greatest number of Orthodox authorities have rejected these arguments (e.g., Joseph Saul Nathanson, Jacob Ettlinger, and Yehiel Weinberg). This rejection, even for consideration as converts, is based upon their ulterior motivation and the likelihood that they will not accept all of the commandments which are not generally observed in the Jewish community today and probably not kept by the Jewish partner (Isaac Herzog, *Heikhal Yitzhaq, Even Haezer* I, #20; Meir Arak, *Imrei Yosher* I, #176; Abraham Kook, *Daat Kohen*, #154; Moses Feinstein, *Igerot Mosheh, Yoreh Deah* I, #157, 160; *Even Haezer* III, #4.

Some Orthodox authorities have ruled that the conduct of a Jewish way of life, even without documentation of conversion, creates a valid assumption of Jewishness (A. Karelitz, *Chazon Ishel, Yev.*, par. 83., #6; *Bet Din Harabanim Hagadol*, Jerusalem, Appeal 1968/26, case of Chanoch and Miriam Langer). Each of these decision was based upon *Talmudic* statements which indicated that this line of thought applied in cases where either father or mother was Jewish (*Yev.* 45b) and conversion was presumed.

Now let us turn to the specifics of your question. Although the Reform Movement has insisted on instruction and intellectual understanding of Judaism, it has never specified precisely how this instruction is to be obtained. Usually, a young convert receives such instruction through Introduction to Judaism classes and reading connected with them. Such classes extend over a period of three months to a year and meet once or several times a week. The reading assignments are usually geared to the intellectual level of the prospective convert. In some instances they include a familiarity with basic books on holidays, liturgy, and history, while others require a thorough knowledge of Jewish history, philosophy, literature, and liturgy. There is nothing which would preclude acquisition of such knowledge over a period of years and in a more informal manner, as the woman described in this question. She has undoubtedly accumulated a considerable body of knowledge through her attendance at services and programs in her synagogue, through random reading, and through constant association with Jewish friends. Certainly, her present knowledge of Judaism would exceed that of anyone who completed the customary introductory courses. Even more important is the fact that her commitment has shown itself to be sincere and has stood the test of time. She not only possesses an intellectual understanding of Judaism, but feels herself Jewish and has involved herself in many aspects of Jewish life both inside and outside the synagogue. From the point of view of knowledge and commitment, we may therefore consider her an appropriate candidate for the final steps of conversion. We should encourage her to move in that direction, especially as she and her husband wish to take this step.

There is nothing in our Reform tradition which demands a public conversion ceremony. Her formal reception into Judaism could take place privately, in the presence of a rabbi and two witnesses.

The prospective convert would be told about *Tevilah* and, in case of a male, about circumcision or *tipat dam*. They should be encouraged to proceed in these directions if that is the custom of the community; however, neither custom is mandatory. It is quite clear from tradition that if such an individual at any time undergoes *Tevilah*, even though not specifically for the purpose of conversion, it would be considered the same as if she had undergone it for that purpose (*Shulhan Arukh, Yoreh Deah* 268.3). This should be considered seriously if the family has any intention of settling in Israel. A Hebrew name of the convert's choice can be appropriately provided at this time as well.

In summary, it would be perfectly possible to accept such a woman as a convert to Judaism with very little further action on her part. This step should be made as easy as possible, and we should do everything in our power to bring *gerei toshav* completely into the sphere of Judaism.

*Walter Jacob, *American Reform Responsa*, New York, 1983, #66.

GERUT AND THE QUESTION OF BELIEF

Walter Jacob

QUESTION: A young woman wishes to convert to Judaism. She has given her reasons for doing so as follows: She will marry a Jewish man and wants to establish a home which shall be unified religiously. She has been impressed by the strength of Jewish family life and by its close-knit unity. Her ethical and moral values coincide with those of Judaism; she is strongly committed to Jewish ethical values, and has considerable interest in Israel and Zionism. She does, however, consider herself agnostic and doubts whether her attitude will change. In all of these matters she is in complete agreement with her Jewish fiance. She feels no attachment to her former Christian background. Can we accept such an individual as a convert to Judaism? (D.O., Pittsburgh, PA)*

ANSWER: The traditional approach to converts was to warn them that they were joining a persecuted community and that many obligations were incumbent upon them. This was followed by a discussion of the ritual necessary for conversion (*Yev.* 46, 47; *Shulhan Arukh, Yoreh Deah* 268; *Yad Hil. Issurei Biah* 15). It is clear that the "obligations" were the *mitzvot* and, of course, it was understood that all of these were of divine origin. Therefore, the source of the *mitzvot* had to be accepted. Modern Orthodox authorities have generally rejected converts who join us for the sake of marriage. Some would accept them in order to avoid the conversion by Reform rabbis (Mendel Kirshbaum, *Menahem Meshiv*, #9), because civil marriage has preceded, or because the couple is living together (David Hoffman, *Melamed Lehoil, Even Haezer* 8, 10; *Yoreh Deah* 85). Similar arguments have been advance by Meshulam Kutner in *Uketora Yaasu,* and by Moses Feinstein in *Igerot Mosheh, Even Haezer* 27. However, the greatest number of Orthodox authorities have rejected these arguments (e.g., Joseph Saul Nathanson, Jacob Ettlinger, and Yehiel Weinberg). Their rejection, even for consideration as converts, was based upon their ulterior motivation and the likelihood that they would not accept all of the commandments which are not generally observed in the Jewish community today and probably not kept by the Jewish partner (Isaac Herzog, *Heichal Yitzchak, Even Haezer* I, #20; Meir Arak, *Imrei Yosher* I, #176; Abraham Kook, *Daat Kohen*, #154; Moses Feinstein, *Igerot Mosheh, Yoreh Deah* I, #157, 160; *Even Haezer* III, #4. It is, therefore, quite clear that in Judaism, belief in God has been considered and was implied as a basis for conversion. The nature of that belief may have varied considerably, as there has always been wide latitude in Judaism and many divergent concepts have been acceptable.

The Biblical figure Ruth has generally been taken as the prototype for all later converts. Her classical statement (Ruth 1:16) mentioned God only at its end, leading some commentators to the conclusion that while rejection of pagan beliefs was considered essential, belief in God might be achieved gradually. The Biblical Book of Job and many of the psalms display questions verging on agnosticism. Some Spanish Jewish philosophers and those of Renaissance Italy expressed similar doubts. Such thoughts were, however, rejected in the more restrictive ghettos of Central and Eastern Europe. In modern times the writings of Mordecai Kaplan, Walter Kaufman, and a host of others have presented a variety of radical positions, sometimes close to agnosticism. Sections of the English prayers in the service of *Gates of Prayer* are written from this questioning stance. Many prospective converts have been and will be motivated by the openness of Judaism which encourages exploration of all ideas even while demanding that the Jewish path of life (*halakhah*) be followed. The woman in question does not deny the existence of God and is not an atheist. We would not have accepted her if she denied the existence of God, but we should accept this convert with the feeling that her attachment to Judaism and the knowledge of it are sufficient to bring her into Judaism and to help her develop a commitment to this religion. As her Jewish life continues, she may also change her views on the nature of God.

*Walter Jacob, *American Reform Responsa*, New York, 1983, #65.

A CONVERT FROM ANOTHER LAND

Walter Jacob

QUESTION: A young woman has come to the United States from Australia. She was converted to Judaism there and possesses the proper documentation; the conversion in this instance seems to have been done rather hurriedly. Should we accept it? She wishes to marry an American Jewish boy. (Robert Gold, Baltimore, MD)*

ANSWER: Unless we have very good reason for rejecting the conversion from a foreign land, we should accept it. Those reasons would primarily deal with the behavior or knowledge of the convert. If the convert's attitude towards Judaism raises doubts, then we are entitled to question the conversion. Otherwise, someone who comes to us with appropriate documentation should be accepted.

We many, of course, suggest further study to the young woman on the grounds that her knowledge of Judaism seems limited. This would make it easier for her to establish a Jewish home and to raise her children within the Jewish community. Such suggestions made in a positive manner, will have the desired effect; they will avoid problems of questioning the efforts of colleagues elsewhere while at the same time maintaining our own standards for conversion.

*Walter Jacob, *Questions and Reform Jewish Answers*, New York, 1992, #127.

CONVERSION AND CHURCH MEMBERSHIP

Solomon B. Freehof

QUESTION: A man wanting to marry a Jewess is willing to go through conversion and join the Jewish congregation, but wishes nevertheless to remain a member of the Christian congregation. What should be the attitude of the Jewish congregation? (Rabbi S. Andhil Fineberg, Mount Vernon, New York.)*

ANSWER: The very fact that such a question arises every now and then these days is an evidence of the modern mood in which sharp distinction between religious groups and traditions tends to grow vague. We Jews, for example, are now accustomed to the thought of having a Jew belong to three or four congregations, each of a different attitude in Judaism. In many cities a man will belong to an Orthodox, a Modern Orthodox, a Conservative, and a Reform congregation. This practice is deemed quite proper and even praiseworthy.

Yet the idea would have been ludicrous a generation or two ago. The responsa of the rabbis of Hungary and Galicia discuss whether Orthodox Jews should associate with the Reformers even in charity, or even whether Orthodox should associate with what might today be called semi-modern Orthodox, the group known in Hungary for historical reasons as the "Status Quo." These "Status Quo" organizations were strictly Orthodox, but the question arose whether one could eat of the *Shehita* of the Status Quo *Shohet*. Possibly it is to the good that the sense of denominational separation has weakened among the Jews. But should we likewise consider it praiseworthy if religious separateness ceases to be sharp between Jews and Christians? And could we contemplate, without disapproval, Jews and Christians belonging to each others' congregations as well as to their own?

Obviously there is a difference between crossing lines that separate Orthodox, Conservative, and Reform Judaism, and crossing lines that separate Judaism and Christianity. Jewish life is undergoing constant change in America. Families have roots in many types of Jewish congregations. The difference in observance is getting less, but between Jews an Christians, although social contacts may increase, the basic theological difference is unshaken. If, as we must assume, belonging to a congregation means accepting its teaching, then a Jew cannot belong to a Christian congregation. Christian congregations are trinitarian and Jewish law prohibits a Jew from adding other divine personages to God in his prayers. Likewise, Christians cannot be part of a Jewish religious community and still be Christians, because they would then have to deny the role of Jesus as Christ.

But it happens that in our present social conditions people contribute to many congregations they do not accept. This is due to our praiseworthy American mood of interdenominational charity. It is therefore quite conceivable that a Christian would want to make a donation to a synagogue, and this is quite in accordance with Jewish law (*Reform Jewish Practice*, II, 45ff). He might consider his dues as merely a charitable contribution. This is, of course, a possibility, but it certainly implies a confusion of theologies.

However, since the case you mention involves the Christian's making himself eligible to be married by a rabbi, then he means his membership in the Jewish congregation to be an evidence of conversion. Conversion is something absolute in the eyes of Jewish law. It is so absolute that the law in the *Talmud* (as codified in the *Shulhan Arukh, Yoreh Deah* 268:9) says that a proselyte is like a newborn babe. He has not even any relatives left in his former life. This is, of course, an overstatement which the law itself modifies. But it means that the division must be clean-cut. (By the way, I am certain that this is the essential meaning of the two or three statements in the Gospels when Jesus speaks to those who would join his movement. He says: "Unless ye are like little children, ye cannot enter the kingdom of heaven." He meant: "Give up all your past and be born anew." This was the classic Jewish concept of conversion.) The man of whom you speak cannot, therefore, either by logic or by the spirit of the law, continue his old affiliations together with the new.

Besides, the *Talmudic* law questions the validity of any conversion entered into merely for the purpose of marriage; it questions its sincerity. If the man involved refuses to give up Christianity, then his acceptance of Judaism cannot possibly be wholehearted or sincere and he cannot be accepted as a proselyte.

So, in spite of the general blurring of boundaries (which is part of the spirit of the age and which also has its good side), nevertheless, on the basis of both common sense and the Jewish law, which requires in conversion a clean-cut separation and unquestionable sincerity, such an arrangement as suggested is utterly unacceptable under Jewish law and tradition.

*Solomon B. Freehof, *Reform Responsa*, Cincinnati, 1960, #18.

MENTAL COMPETENCY OF A CONVERT

Walter Jacob

QUESTION: A prospective convert appears to be mentally unbalanced (paranoid), therefore, his understanding of Judaism is limited. Shall we accept or reject such a convert? (Elizabeth Levine, Congregation Beth-El, Fort Worth, Texas)*

ANSWER: Conversion to Judaism is a major religious step which cannot be taken lightly; this act has legal (*halakhic*) implications. It is clear that Jewish law mandates that anyone acting in a legal capacity must be mentally competent (*Git.* 23a; *Yad Hil. Edut* 9.9; *Shulhan Arukh, Hoshen Mishpat* 188.2). The tradition also demands that any individual engaged in a religious act, especially initially (*lehat-hila*) must be completely mentally competent (*Mishnah* 18, *Rosh Hashanah* 8; *Meg.* 2.4; *Hag.* 1.1; *Men.* 9.8; *Git.* 2.5, etc.). The mentally incompetent and those with other deficiencies could not engage in a valid religious act. If certain kinds of ritual acts had been done by someone mentally incompetent and performed properly, then they were considered acceptable *bediavad*.

The *Talmudic* authorities and the Rabbinic authorities subsequently struggled to achieve a proper definition of mental incompetence and found it as difficult as we in modern times. They, of course, pointed to a variety of strange behavior (*Hag.* 3b; *Nid.* 17a; *Shulhan Arukh, Yoreh Deah* 1.5). Ultimately, this was left to the insight of the presiding judge (*Yad Hil. Edut* 9.9; *Hil. San.* 2.1). These basic decisions were followed by the responsa as well (Isaac b. Sheshet, *Responsa,* #468; Rashbam, *Responsa,* Vol. 2, # 1, etc.), and were not modified in any substantial manner.

The Rabbinic injunction that conversion be carried out before *Bet Din* which shall consist of three members (*Yev.* 46b) makes it clear that this act, although basically religious in nature, is a legal transaction. Therefore, all of the above statements would be applicable. A person who proved to be mentally incompetent, but had been converted to Judaism, is accepted *bediavad*, but certainly not *lehat-hila*.

As a complete understanding of all aspects of Judaism is necessary for a sincere and complete conversion, such prospective converts must be of sound mind and mentally competent. We cannot accept individuals who do not meet these prerequisites.

*Walter Jacob, *American Reform Responsa*, New York, 1983, #67.

THE PREGNANT PROSELYTE

Solomon B. Freehof

QUESTION: A young mother, pregnant, is a candidate for conversion to Judaism. The question asked whether the child which will be born after she had been converted will be a Jewish child by birth, or whether he, too, needs to be converted. (From Rabbi Sherman Stein.)*

ANSWER: The legal status of children of proselytes is discussed under the terms: "conceived in holiness" and "born in holiness." "Holiness" here means Judaism. The status of the child is, to a considerable extent, determined by both of these two tests: A child conceived before the mother is converted and born before the mother's conversion (i.e., neither conceived nor born in "holiness") is a Gentile child and needs separate conversion if it is to be Jewish. A child conceived and born after the mother had converted is completely Jewish and needs no conversion. The child about whom the question is asked here would be described legally as not conceived in holiness, but born in holiness.

The distinction between children conceived before conversion and born after conversion and children conceived after conversion becomes greatly complicated in the case of levirate marriage. If one brother dies childless, does the other brother (both being children of a convert) have to practice levirate marriage or its alternate, *halitzah*? All this is discussed in the *Mishnah* (M. Yevamot, XI:2; the *Talmud* in B. Yevamot 97-98; *Shulhan Arukh*, *Even Haezer* 137:3; and *Yoreh Deah*, 269:3). The fact that the law does not require levirate marriage (or *halitzah*) in such cases is because the levirate marriage depends upon *paternal* relationship, yet even so the law admits that the children have a maternal relationship. In a recent volume of responsa, *Har Tsvi*, #223, by

Tsvi Pesach Frank (Jerusalem, 1964), another question is raised, namely, whether the embryo of a woman being converted may eventually be heir to the property of the mother.

But our chief concern here is not levirate marriage nor inheritance; it is simply whether the child will be born Jewish. As to that question, another principle is involved, one that remains undecided in the literature, namely, whether an embryo is to be considered as merely part of the mother's body (*ubar yerekh imo*) or whether it is an independent personality (cf., the discussion in *Tosfot* to *Sanhedrin* 80b., s.v., "*Ubar*"). The answer to this debated question touches many facets of the law. It applies, for example, to animals. If a pregnant animal is *terefah*, unfit for the altar or for food, is the unborn calf made unfit as part of the mother's body, or not? (*Hulin* 58a) Or, for example, a priestess is not forbidden to go into a cemetery, but there is considerable opinion that a *pregnant* priestess may not go into the cemetery on the chance that her unborn baby may be a male; which, of course, would imply that the embryo in that case is considered to be an independent personality (see the summary of the discussion in *Kol Bo Al Avelut* by Greenwald, p. 76, note 27). This disputed basic question also affects the problem of abortion. If the embryo is actually an independent personality, then abortion would be murder; but if the general principle is upheld that it is merely part of the mother's body, then to save the mother there is no more crime in removing this part of the body than operating on a leg or an arm.

The basic question of whether or not the embryo is merely part of the mother's body would apply specifically to the question asked about the unborn child of a woman being converted. If it is merely part of the mother's body, then with her conversion, all of her including the embryo, is converted. In fact, to some extent this is apparently the fact, because the generally accepted law is that while a man being converted required both circumcision and the ritual bath, this child, all agree, does not require the ritual bath (even if he did need separate conversion) because his mother's ritual bath is deemed to have been effective for him

In *Nimuqei Yosef* (Joseph ibn Chabib) to Chapter 4 of *Yevamot*, near the end of the chapter (bottom of 16a in Vilna editions) there is a discussion of the status of such an embryo, and the opinion of Nachmanides is cited that such an embryo does not require the ritual bath to be converted; and Aaron Halevi adds that when he is born, he is circumcised as any Jewish child is circumcised (i.e., not for the purpose of conversion) and the opinion of Rashi to *Yevamot* 78a is quoted to virtually the same effect.

In other words, the general tendency of the law is to hold that the child does not require ritual bathing and his circumcision is that of a Jewish child (cf. *Yoreh Deah* 268:6 and *Yad, Hil. Issurei Biah* XIII, 7). In general, therefore, it is correct to say that he is converted through the act of his mother's conversion. And, of course, this also applies to a girl child, who could not be circumcised anyhow. In fact, Aaron Halevi indicated that although all male converts require both the ritual bath and circumcision, the male embryo is considered to have had the ritual bath when his mother took it and his conversion is not incomplete on the ground that he is still uncircumcised since he cannot be circumcised at the time, and thus it is analogous to the conversion of a girl baby.

Tzvi Pesach Frank in the responsum mentioned cites the opinion of *Ma'aseh Hiyah* (Hiyah Rofe, Responsum #1, [Safed, died 1620]), which clearly is based on the idea that the mother's conversion completely converts the unborn child. Tsvi Pesach Frank in this responsum (#223, end of column 195) derives the conclusion from Rashi to *Yevamot* 78a that the unborn child of a pregnant proselyte is completely converted by his mother's conversion bath even before he is born. In the next responsum (#224, column 196b) he gives as the opinion of Aaron Halevi and the *Tosfot* that the unborn child is completely a proselyte.

Thus with regard to children conceived as Gentiles and born after the mother is a Jewess (born in *qedusha*) Isserles says that the term "convert" is not to be applied to them (*Darqei Mosheh* to *Tur, Hoshen Mishpat* 33) that they are not converts (but they are born Jews). This is cited by Shach *op. cit.* with approval as the established opinion. That is to say, that while there will be some disagreement as to the child's relationship to previous children of its mother in a possible levirate situation, or whether or not it is too closely related to them to be permitted to be a witness in a Jewish court in cases affecting them (since relatives may not be witnesses) there is no question that the child (though not conceived "in holiness" but born "in holiness") is obligated to fulfill the commandments because it is fully Jewish.

*Solomon B. Freehof, *Modern Reform Responsa*, Cincinnati, 1971, #25.

CONVERTING A MARRIED WOMAN

Solomon B. Freehof

QUESTION: A Jewish man marries a Catholic girl in another country in a Catholic marriage ceremony. Later they come to the rabbi. The woman wants to be converted to Judaism and they want to be married as Jews and pledge to live as Jews. Is there any objection to the rabbi converting the wife and remarrying the couple who had been married previously by a Catholic marriage?*

ANSWER: There is, of course, considerable Orthodox objection to converting to Judaism any non-Jewish woman who has lived with a Jewish man in marriage or common-law marriage or civil marriage, but this objection is not always heeded, and it is certainly the attitude of the Central Conference of American Rabbis to convert women married to Jews.

As for the status of the Catholic marriage, it is clear that we consider Catholic marriage valid for Catholics, but whether it is valid for Jews is a complex question. The problem arose first with the Marranos, many of whom were married in churches and later escaped. Sometimes the woman escaped alone and the husband was killed. Is this woman a perpetual *agunah*, or was the church marriage not a marriage and she therefore free There are two classic responsa on it. One is by Isaac Bar Sheshet. In his Responsum #6 he declares it is no marriage and that the woman is free to be remarried. His younger contemporary and rival in Algiers, Simon ben Zemah Duran, says (Vol. III, #47) that the church marriage is a marriage if there were valid Jewish witnesses present; otherwise it is not. In general, the weight of the authorities is that it is not a valid marriage if a Jew is involved. See the authorities quoted in Freimann, *Seder Qiddushin*, pp.346 ff. For the whole discussion, see the "Report on Mixed Marriage and Intermarriage," *Central Conference of American Rabbis Yearbook*, Vol. 57 (1947).

Actually, the status of a couple's previous marriage is no concern of the rabbi. If a mixed-marriage couple comes before him with the request that the Gentile be converted, if he is convinced that they are both sincere, he certainly may convert a married woman as readily as he might a single woman even though, as mentioned above, some Orthodox authorities would oppose remarrying a woman to a man to whom she had already been married; but on this the Conference is liberal, and many Orthodox rabbis are likewise liberal. Otherwise we would not be able to remarry people who had previously been married by civil authority because the same objection would apply, since they had lived together. It is for the rabbi to satisfy himself that the pledge they make to raise their children as Jewish, to live a Jewish life, is a sincere one. If he is convinced of that, he certainly may convert and marry them. All this is understood as from our more liberal Reform point of view. This is the clear decision of the Conference; see "Report on Mixed Marriage and Intermarriage," from which I quote:

> If, however, the Christian member of the couple desires to convert, we should accept him or her, if sincere, as a candidate for proselytizing. In this regard our attitude would be consistent with that which we take in the case of a mixed civil marriage, in spite of the fact that under such circumstances traditional law would hesitate to accept the convert. Similarly, after conversion we would insist that the couple shall be remarried by a Jewish ceremony. (p. 12)

*Solomon B. Freehof, *Reform Responsa*, Cincinnati, 1960, #19.

CONVERSION OF A YOUNG CHILD

Walter Jacob

QUESTION: What should be done for a four year old who was baptized as a Catholic and born to a Roman Catholic mother? The mother has now married a Jew who has legally adopted her son. Both have agreed that the child should be converted to Judaism and raised as a Jew. He is surgically circumcised. What procedure should this conversion follow? (O.R., Pittsburgh, PA)*

ANSWER: We should begin by reviewing the traditional requirements for conversion. They are clear (*Yev.* 46, 47; *Shulhan Arukh, Yoreh Deah* 268; *Yad Hil. Issurei Biah* 15); a court of three is necessary. Prospective converts must be warned that they are joining a persecuted community and that many new obligations will be incumbent upon them. They were then to bring a sacrifice (in the days when the Temple stood), take a ritual bath, and in the case of males, be circumcised. To this day the requirements of a *bet din, tevilah,* and the *berit* remain for traditional Jews. The sources are clear on the requirements, but considerable discussion about them exists in the *Talmud*. For example, R. Eliezer stated that if a prospective male convert was circumcised, or took a ritual bath, he was considered a proselyte. R. Joshua insisted on both, and his point of view was adopted (*Yev.* 46b). Hillel and Shammai disagreed about a prospective male convert who was already circumcised. *Bet Shammai* insisted that blood must be drawn from him, while *Bet Hillel* stated that one simply accept that circumcision without drawing blood (*Shab.* 135a). The rabbinic authorities decided in favor of *Bet Shammai* (*Shulhan Arukh, Yoreh Deah* 268.1; *Yad Hil. Issurei Biah* 14.5). Clearly, there were differences of opinion about steps necessary for the ritual of conversion in ancient times. The *Talmud* also contains a variety of opinions about the desirability of accepting converts. These reflect historic competition with Christianity, persecution, etc. in the early centuries of our era.

The *Talmudic* discussions insist that the convert must join Judaism without any ulterior motives, and if such are present, the conversion is void (*Yev.* 24b). Of course this opinion applies only prospectively, not retrospective, and *bediavad*, they were accepted. This is hardly at issue here, but let us understand this line of reasoning as well. Some authorities were more lenient in regard to ulterior motives, so Hillel (*Shab.* 31a) readily accepted a convert who stated that he wished eventually to become a high priest. R. Hiya accepted a woman who wanted to marry one of his students (*Men.* 44a). In modern times, although most Orthodox authorities would reject converts who seek to join us for the sake of marriage, some would accept them in order to avoid conversion by Reform rabbis (Mendel Kirshbaum, *Menahem Meshiv*, #9), because civil marriage has preceded, or because the couple is living together (David Hoffman, *Melamed Lehoil, Even Haezer* 8, 10; *Yoreh Deah* 85). Similar arguments have been advanced by Meshullam Kutner in *Uketorah Yaasu* and Moses Feinstein in *Igrot Mosheh* (*Even Haezer* I, 27). However, the greatest number of Orthodox authorities have rejected these arguments (Joseph Saul Nathenson, Jacob Ettlinger, Yehiel Weinberg). Their rejection even for consideration as converts is based upon ulterior motivation and the likelihood that they would not accept all the *mitzvot* as they are generally not observed in the Jewish community today, and probably not kept by the Jewish partner (Isaac Herzog, *Hekhal Yitzhoq, Even Haezer* I, #20; Moses Feinstein, *Igrot Mosheh Yoreh Deah*, I, #157, 160; *Even Haezer* III, #4). I have quoted all of these modern Orthodox authorities to show that our *gerut* may not be accepted by traditional authorities. The Orthodox would, in any case, not accept a liberal conversion. They would consider our *bet din* invalid and would certainly feel that our converts would not have accepted the yoke of the commandments, the entire system of *mitzvot*.

As we view the rite of conversion from a Reform point of view, we should not that the Reform movement has placed its stress on careful instruction with more attention on intellectual rather than ritual requirements. The Central Conference of American Rabbis, in 1892, abolished the requirement of any ritual including circumcision. Most liberal rabbis, however, require circumcision in accordance with the opinion of Hillel (*Shab.* 135b). Converts are to be accepted after due instruction before "any officiating rabbi assisted by no less than two associates." There are, of course, definite limits to instruction in this instance, but some initial education can be undertaken.

Except in a cursory way, no discussion of *tevilah* has been undertaken by liberal Jewish authorities. The custom has fallen into disuse, but was never actually rejected. It is followed for *niddah* by only a small percentage even within the Orthodox community. The practice has been further hindered by endless Orthodox debates about the technical requirements of *miqveh*. A ritual immersion has, therefore, not been considered necessary for conversion in many Reform Jewish communities. There are, however, a number of cities in the United States and Canada in which *tevilah* has been encouraged or required for Reform conversion. In others it is optional.

We might conclude that if the custom possesses meaning for the communities and for the prospective convert, it should be encouraged. This would make it more difficult for traditionalists to challenge liberal conversions, although Orthodox authorities will never willingly accept anything we do as our basic premises differ sharply.

When infants who are adopted become Jewish, it may also be done through the naming ceremony conducted either at home or in the synagogue. In many Reform congregations, this would be considered sufficient ritual conversion for girls and also for a large number of boys. This act, along with Jewish education, would bring the child into the covenant of Judaism in the same manner as a child born Jewish.

We have several possibilities which might be followed in the conversion of this young boy about whom you ask. He should certainly begin to receive some Jewish education. As he is already circumcised, his parents might want to undertake *tipat dam*. Although tradition would encourage this, we would not suggest it for a child four years old. It would certainly provide a negative initial experience with Judaism. However, *tevilah*, with an appropriate ceremony, or a Hebrew name bestowed either in the synagogue or at home, would provide a proper initiation into Judaism through something meaningful and understandable to the young boy and his parents.

*Walter Jacob, *Contemporary American Reform Responsa*, New York, 1987, #49.

CIRCUMCISION OF PROSELYTES

Solomon B. Freehof

QUESTION: Is there any *halakhic* justification for the practice of some Reform groups of accepting adult proselytes without requiring circumcision? (W.V.d.Z., London.)*

ANSWER: The question of whether to admit male proselytes without circumcision was one of the questions which greatly troubled the Reform movement in the United States in its early days. At the second and third sessions of the Central Conference of American Rabbis (1891-1893), the subject was vehemently debated and finally decided by a vote of 25-5 (*CCAR Yearbook*, Vol. III, p. 36), adopting the resolution to accept proselytes without any initiatory rite (i.e., bathing or circumcision).

The debate, which is found chiefly in Vol. II, drew in almost all the leaders of the Reform movement in America. Many of the arguments repeat each other and use the same rabbinical quotations over and over again; but finally the whole question is summed up in the formal report of the Committee signed by Isaac M. Wise himself. This summary is systematic and in many ways original. It is worth epitomizing here because it is as good a statement of the case as has been found anywhere.

The essence of the argument is that there is no actual requirement of an initiatory rite for a proselyte to be found in the Torah; nor is there any definite legal requirement for such a rite found in the *Mishnah*. Therefore the *Talmud* is still debating whether or which initiatory rites are required, and therefore, also, there are some medieval authorities who consider that the initiatory rites are not indispensable.

If this statement can be proved adequately, it is of considerable importance because the Torah has over fifty detailed reference to the *ger*, as to his rights and his privileges and the treatment due him. If, then, in spite of the full Biblical discussion of the *ger*, there is no mention at all of initiatory rites, the silence is eloquent indeed and would certainly tend strongly to prove that actually there were no such rites required. Of course, it was necessary for the Conference Report to explain away the trick which Simeon and Levi played on Shechem and his son Hamor. The action was denounced by Jacob in his blessing. Besides, it was before the giving of the Torah, and, in addition, we do not derive laws from stories or incidents. Next, the statement in Exodus 12:45 must be explained, which says that the *ger* must circumcise all the males of his household before participating in the paschal lamb, "for no uncircumcised may eat of it." This verse does not prove that any initiatory rites were required for the *ger* himself. It means that when the *ger* becomes a Jew, he has the Jewish duty of having his household circumcised. This is proved by the fact that the close of the sentence, "no uncircumcised shall eat of it," means "no uncircumcised *Jew* shall eat of it." See the clear statement in *Targum Jonathan* and Rashi's commentary to the verse. We see, then, that the Torah, which speaks in such detail of the *ger*, never clearly mentions any requirement of initiatory rites when he becomes a Jew.

As for the statement in the report that there is not clear law in the *Mishnah* requiring initiatory rites for *gerim*, there are two passages in the *Mishnah* that need to be explained away. In *Eduyot* 5:2, *Bet Hillel* says, with regard to a *ger*, that to be rid of the foreskin is like escaping from the grave. This is not taken as law, but is just a moral opinion, one which is mentioned only incidentally with regard to other matters. (But, of course, in *Pesachim* 8:8 it is mentioned by *Bet Hillel* more clearly; and it is taken for granted that circumcision is required.) The author of the *Mishnah*, says definitely in a *baraita*, in *Ker.* 9a, that with regard to circumcision *gerim* are like Jews and have this initiatory rite; but the report insists that this is only a *baraita*, and nowhere does Rabbi Judah mention it as a definite law in the *Mishnah*.

There is value, of course, in all this argumentation. It indicates, at least, that there was no legal requirement in Torah and *Mishnah*, only these change, off-hand, and debatable references. Certainly this fact must explain the debate in the *Talmud* itself as to initiatory rites of a proselyte (*Yevamot* 46a and b). There Rabbi Eliezar says that circumcision is the more important of the two rites, and therefore if a proselyte has been circumcised but has not bathed, he is a full-fledged *ger*. Rabbi Joshua, on the other hand, considers the bathing more important and says that if a *ger* has bathed and not been circumcised, he is a full-fledged *ger*.

Then, at the top of 46b, the statement is found that "all agree that if he has not been circumcised, he is full-fledged *ger*"; but further on it says, in the name of Rabbi Yohanan, that he is not a *ger* unless he both bathes and circumcises. So clearly the initiatory rite was still, for a time at least, open to some debate and question.

This explains, perhaps, why in the Middle Ages there were occasional opinions which indicate that circumcision is not a *sine qua non* for the validity of conversion. There is the remarkable statement of the great Jewish polemical writer, Lippman of Mulhausen (14th-15th century), in his *Sefer Nitzahon*. This book, developing as a commentary on the Bible, defending our interpretation of it against Christian charges, makes an unusual statement in the commentary to Genesis 17:10, where the circumcision of males is enjoined upon Abraham as the sign of a covenant. Lippman of Mulhausen refers to the sneering statement of anti-Jews that if it were a covenant, why was not a type of covenant chosen which would include women? To which he makes the following answer: "Our faith does not depend upon circumcision but upon the heart. One [i.e., a candidate for proselytizing] who does not believe sincerely is not converted to Judaism by his circumcision. But one who believes sincerely, is a full Jew even if he is not circumcised."

Some participants in the older Conference debate quote a responsum of the famous rabbi of Constantinople in the fifteenth century, Elijah Mizrachi, in his *Mayyim Amuqim* #27 (the correct reference in the Berlin edition should be #34), in which there is discussion of a Gentile woman and her child who are to be converted, in which he says, with regard to the child, the law *mide-oraita* is that the acceptance of the Torah is sufficient even without bathing or circumcision. (However, he proceeds to say that for adults both rites are required. Still he *does* indicate that according to Torah-law (*mide-oraita*) the rites are not indispensable.) There is an analogous statement in the *Kol Sohol* (*Behinat Ha-qabbalah*) by Leon of Modena. On page 59, where he follows the order of the *Shulhan Arukh*, he speaks about proselytes. He says we ought to give the proselyte the usual explanatory warning and ascertain his sincerity. Then he adds: "We should tell him of the worth of circumcision and its reward. If, then, he wishes to be circumcised, well and good; if not, let him take the ritual bath, and that is sufficient to make him a full Jew in every sense. But when his children are born, he must circumcise them." It is clear, Modena continues, that as for the proselyte himself, the only Biblical drawback to his not being circumcised is that he cannot participate in the paschal offering, but otherwise the Torah makes no mention of circumcision being necessary for a proselyte. (Evidently those who participated in the Conference debate got their chief arguments here. But it is clear that Modena does not give the law as it is, but as he believes it *ought* to be.)

On page 226 of the book *Behinat Ha-Qabbalah*, the editor, Reggio, does not deny that Modena was correct in saying that one can be a full Jew even if uncircumcised (even a *born* Jew, if his lack of circumcision is due to sickness), but he says that circumcision is a vital commandment and should be obeyed (see also p. 230).

All the above debate is significant and must have some bearing on our attitude in the matter of requiring circumcision of proselytes. Nevertheless, there is, I believe, a difference in attitude toward tradition between us and our predecessors. The official report signed by Isaac M. Wise begins with a statement of a basic principle, namely, that our religious life is based upon the Pentateuch. Even though we may interpret it somewhat differently from other Jews, it is the Pentateuch which unites us with the rest of Jewry. In other words, it was the tendency of the early Reformers to go back to origins. Therefore, it was of weighty importance to them that the Bible itself, and also the *Mishnah*, has no clear requirement of initiatory rites for proselytes. I believe that our standpoint is different, though we may not have formulated it as clearly as they did their standpoint. The *total* tradition is vital to us as guidance, at least, if not as rigid governance. Therefore it is important to us that the *Talmud* and Maimonides and the *Shulhan Arukh* (*Yoreh Deah* 268) have circumcision as a firmly established law and that, therefore, it is the widespread practice of our people to circumcise proselytes. The fact that these laws are post-Biblical and post-*Mishnaic* has no strong importance for us, at least not as strong an importance as it did for our predecessors.

Therefore, the matter remains as one for our own decision, based upon our feelings in the matter. The American Reform movement, because of the early decision, has long ceased to insist upon circumcision for proselytes. What English Jewry should do depends upon its conscience. If it seems contrary to the ritual, let them do as we did two generations ago. It might be noted that the

Shulhan Arukh, Yoreh Deah 268:1, says that if the proselyte is mutilated and therefore cannot be circumcised, "the [lack of] circumcision does not prevent his conversion, and it is enough if he takes the ritual bath." It is also a fact nowadays that most male infants, whether Jew or Christian, are circumcised by the obstetrician; therefore there are very few actually uncircumcised, or at least less of them, among would-be converts. It might be a worthwhile decision on the part of the English Reformers not to insist upon taking "the drop of blood of the covenant" if a convert is already circumcised (cf. the discussion of Asher b. Jehiel to the passage in *Yevamot*). If the English Reform movement decides to give up the requirement of circumcision, the fact that the Bible and the *Mishnah* have no such clear requirement, and the fact that this has been the practice of American Reform almost from the beginning, might aid them to the decision. If they wish to insist upon the requirement, then perhaps they will waive the requirement of taking the drop of blood from one already circumcised.

ADDENDUM

Since writing the above, I have come across an interesting discussion of the question in the responsa *Hazon La-moed* by Mordecai Dov Eidelberg, who was rabbi in Nickolayev, Russia. The book was printed in Bialystok in 1923. The problem that confronted him was this: A Russian officer was converted to Judaism by a well-known rabbi. The officer, however, was not circumcised at the conversion because he was not well at the time. He promised to be circumcised at a later date when he would be restored to health. The rabbi who converted him insisted that under these circumstances the officer was a full proselyte even though he was not yet circumcised.

The problem came before Rabbi Eidelberg because the convert was to marry a young woman in Rabbi Eidelberg's congregation. The rabbi, therefore, had to decide whether he agreed with the converting rabbi that a man can be a full proselyte without circumcision. He discusses the question of hemophiliacs and diabetics, for whom the operation might be a grave danger, and also the question of a mutilated person who cannot be circumcised. Can such individuals ever be considered full converts? He ends his responsum by saying that the matter of conversion without circumcision can be argued either way and needs final decision by the leading scholars of our time, and so he refuses at present to make a decision and act upon it. The responsum is #7. However, David Hoffman, in *Melamed L'ho-il*, *Yoreh Deah* 86, says forthrightly that he would not convert any man who is too sick to be circumcised.

*Solomon B. Freehof, *Reform Responsa for Our Time*, Cincinnati, 1977, #15.

PROSPECTIVE CONVERT WHO FEARS CIRCUMCISION

Walter Jacob

QUESTION: Is there any precedent in the *halakah* for a prospective convert who fears circumcision to avoid it? Similarly, is there a precedent for a prospective convert who has a deeply-rooted fear of water? Must he/she proceed with the requirement for *Miqveh*? (Rabbi Lawrence A. Englander, Mississauga, Ontario)*

ANSWER: The traditional requirements for conversion are clear (*B. Yev.* 46, 47; *Shulhan Arukh, Yoreh Deah* 268; *Yad, Hil. Issurei Biah* 15). A court of three is necessary, and prospective converts must be warned that they are joining a persecuted community and that many new obligations will be incumbent upon them. In the days when the Temple stood, they were to bring a sacrifice, take a ritual bath, and -in the case of males -be circumcised. To this day, the requirements of a *Bet Din, Tevilah*, and *Berit* remain for traditional Jews. Sources are clear on the requirements, but considerable discussion about them exists in the Talmud. For example, R. Eliezer stated that if a prospective male convert was circumcised or took a ritual bath, he was considered a proselyte. R. Joshua insisted on bath, and his point of view was adopted (*Yev.* 46b). Hillel and Shammai disagreed about a prospective male convert who was already circumcised. *Bet Shammai* insisted that blood must be drawn from him, while *Bet Hillel* stated that one may simply accept the circumcision without drawing blood (*Shab.* 135a). The Rabbinic authorities decided in favor of *Bet Shammai* (*Shulhan Arukh, Yoreh Deah* 268.1; *Yad, Hil. Issurei Biah* 14.5). Clearly, there were differences of opinion about the steps necessary for the ritual conversion in ancient times. As is well known, the *Talmud* also contains a variety of opinions about the desirability of accepting converts. These reflect the historic competition with Christianity, persecution, etc. in the early centuries of our era.

As we view the rite of conversion from a Reform point of view, we should not that the Reform Movement has placed its stresson careful instruction, with more attention to intellectual rather than ritual requirements. The Central Conference of American Rabbis in 1892 abolished the requirement of any ritual, including circumcision. Most Liberal rabbis, however, require circumcision or accept the existing circumcision (in accordance with the opinion of Hillel in *Shab.* 135b). Converts were to be accepted after due instruction before "any officiating rabbi assisted by no less than two associates." There has been very little discussion of *tevilah* by Liberal Jewish authorities. The custom has fallen into disuse, but was never actually rejected by Liberal Judaism. There are a number of cities in the United States and Canada in which *tevilah* has been encouraged or required for Reform conversion, as there has been cases of *tevilah* undertaken at the express wish of the prospective convert.

Immersion in a *miqveh* should not prove particularly difficult, however. The *miqveh* itself need contain only forty *seah* of water, which is approximately a hundred and twenty gallons, and must be about four feet in depth, so that a person can easily submerge himself completely (*Sifra* 6.3; *Yoma* 31a, *Er.* 4b). During most of the conversion procedure the convert would be in water up to his/her neck, and then for an instant be completely submerged. In other words, as we are not discussing a deep body of water or an extensive one, it should not be much more difficult than entering a bath; therefore, someone with a phobia about water should be able to undergo the ritual. However, as it is only rarely used for Reform conversion, we can dispense with it for such a convert even in a community where it is usually utilized.

Theoretically, circumcision may be viewed similarly according to the statement of the Central Conference of American Rabbis of 1892. In practice, circumcision has, however, been a virtually universal requirement. It may be made easier, especially for an adult or an older child, by providing an anesthetic. The early authorities of the last generation were against using an anesthetic (Meir Arik, *Imrei Yosher II*, 140). This was part of the rejection of all innovations, but more recent authorities have not hesitated to approve the use of an anesthetic (J.L. Zierelsohn, *Maarchai Lev*, 53; Gedalia Felder, *Nahalat Tzevi*, p. 57). When the operation is done on a new-born child, it is presumed that the nervous system does not yet fully convey a sense of pain, but as that is not true of an adult or an older child, anesthetic may alleviate the pain and remove the fear of the impending operation. Circumcision may, of course, be postponed indefinitely due to health reasons, and we might consider the phobia as such a health reason. In this way, one could also assure the convert that he would be acceptable even without circumcision.

The prospective convert should be encouraged to undergo circumcision although, strictly speaking, this requirement may also be waived according to the earlier Reform decision.

*Walter Jacob, *American Reform Responsa*, New York, 1983, #69.

A CONVERT AND HEBREW

Walter Jacob

QUESTION: A middle aged convert is hesitant about conversion. She has given up all identity with Christianity, studied Judaism diligently to the best of her ability, and has learned enough to qualify as a convert. She feels that she is ready and the rabbi also indicated that conversion is now possible. She has, however, hesitated to take this step on the grounds that she knows very little Hebrew, has no linguistic aptitude, and feels that she can not be a good Jewess without a firm grasp of Hebrew. Would we agree with her or would we state that Hebrew is not essential? (Tillie Lebowitz, Tulsa, OK)*

ANSWER: The Hebrew language has played an important role in Jewish life throughout our history. Through the ages we have done our best to encourage the study of Hebrew; our greatest literature has been written in Hebrew or Aramaic.

Within the Reform movement we have put less emphasis on Hebrew and more on the vernacular in our services, in order to enable the worshipper to understand the service fully. Yet we retain a considerable amount of Hebrew in the liturgy.

Problems with understanding the Hebrew language go back to the end of the Biblical period. A large portion of our people were no longer familiar with Hebrew, even in the time of Ezra and Nehemiah (*Neh.* 8:8), so the Scriptural reading had to be translated for them. By the time of the *Mishnah*, the common people no longer used Hebrew, therefore, the *shema*, *tefilah*, and the *birkhat hamazon* were permitted in the vernacular (*M. Sotah* 7.1). This, then, also was the later decision of the *Talmud* (*Sotah* 32b ff); it enabled individuals who recited petitions to pray sincerely and with full knowledge of what they were saying. A parallel stand was taken by later authorities, so the *Sefer Hassidim* of the eleventh century (#588 and #785) stated that those who did not understand Hebrew should pray in the vernacular. Maimonides provided a similar statement (*Yad Hil. Ber* 1.6), while the *Tur* and *Shulhan Arukh* made a distinction between private and public prayers. Private prayers were preferably said in Hebrew. While congregational prayers might be recited in the vernacular. They expressed a preference but did not exclude the vernacular in either instance (*Tur Orah Hayyim* 101; *Shulhan Arukh, Orah Hayyim* 101.4). Aaron Chorin, Eliezer Lieberman and others, who defended the changes made by the Reform movement in the last century and its use of the vernacular, however, insisted that a number of prayers should continue to be recited in Hebrew (*Qinat Ha-emet*; *Or Nogah* Part I). Of course, they felt that nothing stood in the way of using the vernacular.

In most conversion courses the study of a minimal amount of Hebrew is encouraged, although with the limited amount of time available real familiarity with the language is impossible. In many instances the convert will be able to read simple prayerbook Hebrew and know the meaning of a text by association. The continuation of Hebrew studies has always been encouraged but is not a mandatory part of the conversion process. We would therefore, say to this individual that a minimum knowledge of Hebrew will be helpful for familiarity with religious services and as an association with tradition. More advanced knowledge of the Hebrew is desirable, but may not be possible for everyone. The sincerity of this convert is enough to lead to her acceptance. She should be assured that a fuller knowledge of Hebrew is not required of her. We will welcome her with the hope that she will be a good addition to our people.

*Walter Jacob, *Questions and Reform Jewish Answers*, New York, 1992, #126.

THE *MIQVEH* AND REFORM CONVERTS

Walter Jacob

QUESTION: Has liberal Judaism taken a position of the use of a *miqveh* as part of the conversion ceremony to Judaism? Should this ancient custom be reintroduced? (Simon Levy, Harrow-on-the-Hill, England)*

ANSWER: The traditional requirements for conversion are clear (*Yeb.* 46, 46; *Shulhan Arukh Yoreh Deah* 268; *Yad Hil. Issurei Biah* 15); a court of three is necessary. Prospective converts must be warned that they are joining a persecuted community and that many new obligations will be placed upon them. They were then to bring a sacrifice in the days when the Temple stood, take a ritual bath, and in the case of the males, be circumcised. To this day the requirements of a *beit din*, *tevilah* and *berit* remain for traditional Jews. The sources are clear on the requirements, but considerable discussion about them exists in the *Talmud*. For example, R. Eliezer stated that if a prospective male convert was circumcised or took a ritual bath, he was considered a proselyte. R. Joshua insisted on both and his point of view was adopted (*Yev.* 46b); Hillel and Shammai disagreed about a prospective male convert who was already circumcised; *Bet Shammai* insisted that blood must be drawn for him, while *Bet Hillel* stated that one may simply accept that circumcision without drawing blood (*Shab.* 135a). The rabbinic authorities decided in favor of *Bet Shammai* (*Shulhan Arukh, Yoreh Deah* 268.1; *Yad Hil. Issurei Biah* 14.5). Clearly there were differences of opinion about steps necessary for the ritual of conversion in ancient times. These may reflect historic competition with Christianity, persecution, etc., in the early centuries of our era.

The *Talmudic* discussions insist that the convert must join Judaism without any ulterior motives, and if such are present, the conversion is void (*Yev.* 24b). Of course this opinion applies only prospectively, not retrospectively and *bedi-avad* they were accepted.

Some authorities were more lenient in regard to ulterior motives, so Hillel (*Shab.* 31a) readily accepted a convert who stated that he wished eventually to become a high priest. R. Hiya accepted a woman who wanted to marry one of his students (*Men.* 44a). In modern times, although most Orthodox authorities would reject converts who seek to join us for the sake of marriage, some would accept them in order to avoid the conversion by Reform rabbis (Mendel Kirshbaum, *Menahem Meshiv* #9), because civil marriage has preceded or because the couple is living together (*Yoreh Deah* 85). Similar arguments have been advanced by Meshullam Kutner in *Uketorah Yaasu*, Mosheh Feinstein (*Igerot Mosheh, Even Haezer*, Vol. 1, #27). However, the greatest number of Orthodox authorities have rejected these arguments (Joseph Saul Nathenson, Jacob Ettlinger, Yehiel Weinberg). Their rejection was based upon ulterior motivation and the likelihood that they would not accept all the commandments especially as they are not generally observed in the modern Jewish community and probably not kept by the Jewish partner (Isaac Herzog, *Hekhal Yizhaq, Even Haezer*, Vol. 1, #20; Meir Arak, *Imrei Yosher*, Vol. 1, #176; Abraham Kook, *Daat Kohen*, #154; Mosheh Feinstein, *Igrot Mosheh Yoreh Deah*, Vol. 1, #157, 160; *Even Haezer* III, #4).

I have quoted all of these modern Orthodox authorities to show that our future path in this matter should not be based on the false assumption of bringing grater unity to the Jewish community. The Orthodox would, in any case, not accept a liberal conversion; they would consider our *Bet Din* invalid and would certainly feel that our converts have not accepted the yoke of the commandments.

As we view the rite of conversion from a Reform point of view, we should note that the Reform movement has stressed careful instruction with more attention to intellectual rather than ritual requirements. The Central Conference of American Rabbis, in 1892, abolished the requirement of any ritual including circumcision. Most liberal rabbis, however, require circumcision or accept the existing circumcision in accordance with the opinion of Hillel (*Shab.* 135b). Converts were to be accepted after due instruction before "any officiating rabbi assisted by no less than two associates."

Except in a cursory way, no discussion of *tevilah* has been undertaken by liberal Jewish authorities. The custom has fallen into disuse, but was never actually rejected by liberal Judaism. Ritual immersion has completely ceased to be practiced for *nidah* and is followed only by a small percentage within the Orthodox community. The practice has further been hindered by endless Orthodox debates about the technical requirements of the *miqveh*. A ritual immersion has, therefore, not been considered necessary for conversion among most Reform Jewish communities. There are, however, a number of cities in the United States and Canada in which *tevilah* has been encouraged or required for Reform conversions.

We might conclude that if the custom possesses meaning for the community and for the prospective convert, it should be encouraged. This would make it more difficult for traditionalists to challenge liberal conversions, although Orthodox authorities will never willingly accept anything we do as our basic premises differ sharply.

*Walter Jacob, *Contemporary American Reform Responsa*, New York, 1987, #44.

A SWIMMING POOL AS A *MIQVEH*

Walter Jacob

QUESTION: May a swimming pool be used as a *miqveh*? What are the requirements for immersion which we would follow with converts in those communities in which ritual immersion is indicated or where the rabbi feels strongly about the inclusion of this ritual? (Rabbi D. Shapiro, White Plains, NY)*

ANSWER: We will deal briefly with the question of the use of the *miqveh* for conversion in Reform *gerut* as that has been dealt with in earlier responsa ("Origin of the *Miqveh* for Conversion" and "The *Miqveh* and the Reform Convert"). The question of rituals which should be used to accept converts was debated in Germany in the eighteen-forties. This centered mainly around the requirement of circumcision (*milah*). Samuel Holdheim and the Reform Society were opposed to circumcision. Abraham Geiger and the vast majority emphasized it as a necessary rite. The issue was raised in America at the Philadelphia Conference of 1869 and again at the Pittsburgh meeting in 1885; between these conferences various Reform rabbis had written pamphlets and articles on the question. *Tevilah* was not debated and only generally included in these discussions. This was equally true in 1893 when considerable time was spent on debating "Initiatory Rites of Proselytes." The resolution which was passed called for acceptance of proselytes "without any initiatory rite" (*C.C.A.R. Yearbook*, Vol. III, p. 36). Those rabbis who recorded the reason for their opposition to the resolution dealt only wit *milah*, not *tevilah*.

The ritual of *tevilah*, therefore, quietly vanished without debate; it has similarly reappeared on the scene as a larger number of American Reform rabbis have made *tevilah* optional or mandatory for *gerut*. In many instances the traditional *miqveh* has been used. When none was available, immersion has taken place elsewhere. Let us turn to the requirements for a *miqveh*.

We should begin with the regulations connected with a traditional *miqveh* which are clear. It should be at least three cubits long, a cubit wide, and a cubit deep and contain forty seahs of water (*Er.* 4b; *Yoma* 31a; *Shulhan Arukh, Yoreh Deah* 201.1). In other words, a space which contains between 171 and 191 gallons of water would be sufficient.

The water must be from a natural source. It may be form a spring, a lake or a river which has been fed by a natural spring in accordance with a statement in Leviticus (11.36): "Nevertheless a fountain or a cistern wherein is a gathering of water shall be clean." The opening word of that statement has been interpreted to be restrictive (*akh*) according to tradition (*Hul* 84a; *Sifra* to Lev. 11.36). Rain water is also appropriate as is water melted from ice or snow (*M. Miq.* 7.1; *Yad Hil. Miqvaot* 3.1 ff; *Shulhan Arukh, Yoreh Deah* 201.2; 201.30).

It is clear from the rabbinic sources that the only usable liquid is water (*Shulhan Arukh, Yoreh Deah* 201.23) and that it must be still water (*Sifra* to Lev. 11.36; Rashi to *Shab.* 65b, to *Nid.* 67a; *Tos.* to *Hag.* 11a; *Yad Hil. Miqvaot* 10.16; *Shulhan Arukh, Yoreh Deah* 201.2). The water which enters the *miqveh* may not be drawn or poured into it (*Smag* Positive Commandment #248; *Tos.* to *B.B.* 66b, to *Pes.* 17b; *Shulhan Arukh Yoreh Deah* 201.3). It must enter through a system of pipes not subject to uncleanliness; this excludes pipes of metal, wood or clay unless specifically treated to turn them into "vessels" (*Rosh Miq.* 5.12; *Yad Hil. Miq.* 5.5; *Shulhan Arukh Yoreh Deah* 201.34; *Hatam Sofer Responsa Yoreh Deah* 199). The *miqveh* itself must be constructed in the ground or be located in a building which is built into the ground. The *miqveh* may not consist of a tub (*B.B.* 66b; *Tos.* to *Pes.* 17b; *Shulhan Arukh, Yoreh Deah* 201.6).

We should also note that if a pool has attained the status of a *miqveh*, then one may add any amount of water, such as tap water, by other means and the *miqveh* does not lose its status. Furthermore, the original *miqveh* may be connected with another through a pipe. If this is done and it flows into the neighboring pool it is considered and appropriate *miqveh* (Rashi to *Yeb.* 47b).

The main problem in building a *miqveh* are the rules connected with the piping, and the vessels through which the water must pass. The vessels can not be of such a size that objects can be placed into them; the pipe itself is not considered a vessel (*M. Miq.* 4.1; *Yad Hil. Mikvaot* 6.1). The problem of using a modern water system are the reservoirs, holding tanks, and filters, through which spring or river water flows before reaching the user. Most *miqvaot* in modern cities, therefore, use rain or melted snow water as the basic supply to which other water is added as needed (*Shulhan Arukh, Yoreh Deah* 201.36; Ezekiel Landau, *Noda Biyehuda Yoreh Deah* 136, 137; *Hatam Sofer Responsa* #198, #199, #203ff; *Rosh Responsa* #30, #31).

Now let us turn to the matter of a swimming pool seen in a traditional setting. It is clear from the outset that in many ways a swimming pool satisfies the provisions of a *miqveh*. Most pools are built into the ground or into buildings which are in the ground. There would be no difficulty of properly guiding two hundred gallons of rain water or melted snow into the pool at the outset and then adding other water. Similarly a small neighboring splash pool could be properly prepared and connected. The problem of recirculated water which causes a flow and drainage holes in the bottom of the pool are among the chief obstacles for traditional Jews in using a swimming pool as a *miqveh*. This is true even though the flow of water is entirely internal as the pumps pass water through the filters and return it to the pool. For a complete discussion of these problems see Benjamin Kreitman, "May a

Swimming Pool Serve as a Kosher *Miqveh*," (*Proceedings of the Rabbinical Assembly*, Vol. 33, 1969, pp. 219 ff). The nineteenth and twentieth century traditional authorities have turned more and more to technical discussions about the *miqveh* and even questioned the appropriateness of *miqvaot* in long use. For our purposes these details upon details are irrelevant.

We must ask about the purpose of this ritual. If we return to the Biblical and early rabbinic statements connected with purification for *gerut* or other purposes, we can see that the authorities sought a ritual which used pure water in an appropriate setting. This symbolic purification changed the status of the individual involved (*Yad Hil. Miqvaot* 4.1, 11.12). This symbolism is meaningful to many modern converts as it helps them to make the transition to Judaism.

Symbolic purification for *gerut* can be properly provided by a natural body of water, a *miqveh* or a swimming pool. If a pool is used, the ritual should take place only when no other use is made of it. The ceremony should be conducted in an appropriately dignified manner.

We should remember that our use of *tevilah* for *gerut* has gradually developed among us as we have changed since 1893. No rituals have been mandated by the Central Conference of American Rabbis which stipulated that acceptance of Judaism occur before a rabbi and two associates for *gerut*; however, both *milah* and *tevilah* have been widely used.

*Walter Jacob, *Contemporary American Reform Responsa*, New York, 1987, #45.

THE INCOMPLETE CONVERSION

Solomon B. Freehof

QUESTION: A young lady who is studying in preparation for conversion to Judaism must leave the city to join her husband-to-be at an army camp. The rabbi decided that even though the course of instruction has not yet been completed, he would convert her immediately and marry her Jewishly, provided she will accept the responsibility of completing her training under the guidance of the rabbi of the city where the army camp is located. Does this decision comport with the spirit of Jewish law? (Rabbi Allen H. Podet, Seattle, Washington.)*

ANSWER: Although the *Shulhan Arukh* (*Yoreh Deah* 268) gives complete and detailed description of the method of converting a Gentile to Judaism, nevertheless it is evident that there is considerable doubt as to whether conversion necessarily requires the completion of the entire process described. If it does not necessarily require the entire process, then at which point in the uncompleted process may the candidate be considered to be a proselyte?

It is noteworthy that even at the early stage of the development of the law there was some dispute on basic parts of the process. The law is that a candidate for conversion has to be circumcised and take the ritual bath and bring a sacrifice to the Temple. The latter requirement is still mentioned by Maimonides (*Yad, Hil. Issurei Biah* 13:5) who considers that the proselyte still owes the sacrifice, to be given when the Temple is rebuilt. But as for the other two elements, there is a dispute in *Yevamot* 46a between Rabbi Elazar and Rabbi Joshua. Rabbi Elazar says that if circumcised but not ritually bathed, he is a complete proselyte. Rabbi Joshua says that if bathed but not circumcised, he is nevertheless a full proselyte.

Of course the final decision is (46b) that he must be both circumcised and bathed; and a woman proselyte, of course, must have the ritual bath. As the law is now in the *Shulhan Arukh*, the proselyte is first closely asked why he is willing to accept the persecutions, etc., to which Jews are subjected. Then he is told of the reward and punishment for some of the commandments, and then he is circumcised and, when healed, taken to the ritual bath.

Now we should try to determine the degree of importance of these elements in the process: a) the questioning as to sincerity, b) the instruction in the commandments, c) the double ritual requirements. As for the second (the instruction in the commandments) the law is careful to say: You do not do more than mention "some" (*mitzvot*) of the commandments. You do not tell him too many (*en marbin alav*). In other words, it is clear that the instruction in the law is the least important of the three elements, perhaps because the law is so complex that you could not instruct him sufficiently anyhow. Furthermore, even the instruction mentioned is not actually instruction. The laws are cited to show what punishment there is for their violation. The candidate is told that while he is a Gentile, he will *not* be punished for violation of these laws, but when he becomes a Jew, he *will* be punished. So why is he willing to take this new burden on himself? Therefore it is evident that even this partial instruction in the law is not so much instruction, but belongs under the first element mentioned, namely, the testing of his sincerity.

Even the earnest testing of sincerity was subject to some mitigation. Doubt as to sincerity was based upon the desire to improve one's status or increase one's safety or to marry a Jew. It is because of the first two doubts that the *Talmud* deprecates the converts who flocked to Judaism in the time of David and Queen Esther. And it is because of the latter doubt, the desire to marry a Jew, that many Orthodox rabbis hesitate to perform conversions today. Yet this doubt as to motive of the candidate occurred in the case of Hillel and in the case of Rabbi Hiya (*Shabbat* 31a and *Menahot* 44a). In one case the proselyte wanted to become high priest some day and in the other, the proselyte wanted to marry a Jew. Yet in both cases the candidates were accepted, and the explanation is give (see *Tosfot* to *Yevamot* 24b, s.v. "*Lo*") that they were accepted because these two scholars were confident of their judgment that these two proselytes would be sincere proselytes despite their present motives. In fact, Joseph Caro, in his *Bet Yosef* to the *Tur* (*Yoreh Deah* 268) uses a guiding phrase: "It all depends upon the judgement of the court" (*hakol lefi re'ut bet din*). So the *Shulhan Arukh* itself (268:12) says that if a man has been circumcised and bathed, then he is a full proselyte, even though there is ground to believe that he converts for the sake of marriage.

We may conclude that in Orthodox law the order of importance is, first, the ritual circumcision and bathing; second, the question of sincerity; and third, and least important, instruction.

With us in the Reform movement, we have made a clear-cut change. We have declared that the ritual (circumcision and ritual bath) will not be binding upon us. We have made the question of sincerity important, but have declared (see Conference Report on "Mixed Marriage and Inter-Marriage," page 8) that the desire of the couple to marry is not to be considered proof of the insincerity of the conversion, but perhaps the very reverse. We have placed our main emphasis on the instruction.

Now the same question comes to us which confronted Orthodox law: How much or how little of the process is indispensable? Or whether, under special circumstances, the candidate can be converted before the usual course is finished, on condition that the course be continued after marriage, either with the rabbi or with another. The answer must be given in light of

Joseph Caro's summation: "It depends upon the judgement of the *bet din*." If the rabbi believes that this is a sincere person who will maintain the affiliation with Judaism and that her willingness to continue instruction even after the marriage is a further evidence of her sincerity, then he may certainly shorten the period of instruction, especially when this is done temporarily.

But there is need for caution. Inasmuch as it is the instruction which has become the most important element for us, we must guard it carefully and not let it become a mere formality, lest it come down eventually to a few words of instruction in one interview and the candidate then be considered to be converted. If the shortening of the course is done in exceptional cases only and there is good reason for it, and if thereby the general practice of the instruction of proselytes is not by this one case weakened, then there is no reason why the rabbi may not use his judgment in the matter.

*Solomon B. Freehof, *Modern Reform Responsa*, Cincinnati, 1971, #27.

LAYMAN CONDUCTING A CONVERSION

Solomon B. Freehof

QUESTION: An Indian Gentile girl in Bombay desires to convert to Judaism. She has presented herself as a candidate for conversion to our Reform congregation in Bombay (a congregation of the *Benei Israel*). The congregation has no rabbi at present and they have asked whether laymen are eligible to perform the ceremony of conversion.*

ANSWER: The *Shulhan Arukh* in *Yoreh Deah* 268:3 says that a conversion must be conducted by a court of three "eligible to judge." The question which concerns us is what is meant by this phrase. Of course, "eligible to judge" can mean simply that the judges are not relatives. (See *Perishah* to the *Tur* who quotes the Mordecai as the sources of this explanation.) However, there is a much more fundamental question involved as to the nature of the court.

In *Mishnaic* and *Talmudic* times there were two classes of courts, those that dealt with religious and criminal matters and those that dealt with adjudicating civil disputes. The courts that dealt with religious and criminal matters were generally the fixed courts and were composed of men who were formally ordained (*musmakhim*). Since ordination in the old classic sense could take place only in Palestine, then those who conducted such courts in Babylon had a somewhat different status, but one which amounted to the same thing. They were called *mumhim*, literally "skilled men." It meant, actually, official appointees of the Exilarch. *Musmakhim* in Palestine and *mumhim* in Babylon could also judge civil matters; but civil matters could legally be judged by amateurs if the two parties in dispute selected them and were content with each other's selection.

In post-*Talmudic* times official ordination (or in Babylon, official appointment) has ceased. Our present *semikhah* is merely the use of an old name; it is actually only a license to teach, although it uses the formula "he may judge." Modern rabbis considered that their right to judge in certain cases, which in the past required official judges, inheres in the fact that they are agents of the judges of the past. Now our question really amounts to this: Is conversion one of those religious functions which in the past would require official judges and therefore now require "ordained" rabbis who are deemed to be their direct agents, or is it rather akin in status to such civil matters which even in the past could be adjudicated by laymen?

The fullest discussion of the question of conversion is found in the *Talmud* in *Yevamot* 46 and 47. The *Talmud* concludes at the bottom of 46b that the incident described on that page proves that a court of three is required for conversion. Then it raises but rejects the supposition that the court must be composed of *mumhim*, learned officials. However, although *mumhim* were not required for conversion in those days, it nevertheless may be that nowadays scholars (*talmidei hahamim*) may nevertheless be required and that ordinary laymen are ineligible. There are certain functions which for various reasons came to be restricted to scholars (therefore generally rabbis), for example, matters of marriage or divorce, or matters of releasing vows, etc. Is conversion to be considered such a matter which today must be left to scholars (i.e., rabbis)?

The *Talmud* in *Qiddushin* 62a and 62b gives a discussion which begins with the question of heave offering, starting with the statement that a man may not give heave offering from fruit that is still unharvested for fruit that is already harvested. It then moves to a discussion of whether a man may say to a woman, "I hereby marry you, the marriage to take effect after I have become (or after you have become) a proselyte." Then the discussion continues as follows: "But surely to become a proselyte is within his power to achieve" (and therefore the marriage proposal would be valid) and the *Talmud* answers, "No; it is not necessarily within his power to achieve because a proselyte needs three people because the word *mishpat* is used with regard to it, as with civil cases which require three." Then the *Talmud* says, "How does he know that he will be able to find three who will assemble to convert him" Rashi simply explains this as saying he may not find three Israelites to gather to go through with the process.

It is clear from this discussion and Rashi's commentary that any three Israelites are authorized to perform the conversion, and the *Tosfot* to the place addresses itself exactly to this question and comes to the same conclusion, and quotes Rabbi Nathaniel to the same effect, that conversion does not require trained and official personnel.

Benjamin Zeev (sixteenth century) in his Responsa I, 72, quotes the responsum of Isaac the son of Samuel to the effect that conversion is valid even if conducted by three *hedyotot* (i.e., three ordinary unlearned laymen). Benjamin Zeev concludes with the general statement that in matters of conversion, we ought to follow the line of leniency and therefore should, if necessary, allow three ordinary men to conduct the conversion, less we "lock the doors in the face of converts." The phrase is from *Tosfot, Yevamot* 47a. However, Zvi Hirsch Chayes of Zolkiev, who lived about a hundred years ago, says that it is preferable that the three men be scholars. See his notes to the *Talmud* to *Shabbat* 46b (the notes are to be found at the back of the large Vilna edition.)

Benjamin Zeev's general principle that in matters of conversion we should be lenient rather than too strict is revealed in the summary of the law as found in the *Shulhan Arukh, Yoreh Deah* 268. There we are told that while a court of three is required, nevertheless if a person is converted before two, the conversion is valid as a *fait accompli* (*bedi-avad*), although not as a preferred procedure. So, too, while the whole conversion process must be consciously directed with full understanding of the implications, nevertheless a formal bathing for some other purpose than conversion can be considered valid for conversion as a *fait accompli*. All these opinions are based upon earlier legal decisions. Besides the clear evidence of the preference for leniency in this matter, the *Shulhan Arukh* also reveals the uncertainty as to the types of judges required. Whereas in 268:3 it merely says "three men who are eligible to judge," i.e., not relatives, nevertheless when the words of admonition are repeated after the ritual bath (in 268:1) Isserles adds to the statement that it must be scholars who give him the final instruction. However, the *Shulhan Arukh* in 268:12 sums it up by saying that if he were circumcised and bathed in the presence of three *hedyotot* (i.e., three average men) he is fully a *ger*.

Ben Zion Uziel, the late Sephardic Chief Rabbi, in his very last book of Responsa *Mishp'tei Uziel, Even Haezer* 13, p. 54, Jerusalem, 1964 says: "It is the *halakhah*, as we learn from the words of the Rambam, that the reception of proselytes does not require a *Bet Din* of skilled men, but even with three ordinary men (*hedyotot*) it is quite sufficient."

In brief, the general mood of leniency has led the majority of the authorities cited and the *Shulhan Arukh* itself to conclude that any three laymen can legally conduct the conversion. However, since the people are of the *Benei Israel*, this woman and her husband (after she has been converted and married) may move to Israel, and since the Orthodox rabbinate in Israel generally refuses to accept conversion by a Reform rabbi on the ground that the requisite bathing has not been performed, it would be advisable to have three men send in a woman with her to the *miqveh* to have her fulfill this ritual requirement.

*Solomon B. Freehof, *Current Reform Responsa*, Cincinnati, 1969, #25.

PRIVACY OF A CONVERT

Walter Jacob

QUESTION: The congregation keeps a public register in its library of all the life cycle events such as birth, *Bar/Bat Mitzvah*, confirmations, marriages, and deaths. All conversions are also included. Does such a public register of conversions invade the privacy of the convert? Is it appropriate to maintain it in the congregational library? (Rabbi J. Edelstein, Monroeville, PA)*

ANSWER: Conversion in Judaism is a public rite conducted before a court of three (*Yev.* 47b; *Yad Hil. Issurei Biah* 13.14, *Shulhan Arukh, Yoreh Deah* 268, 269). Such requirements obviously makes it initially a public act and assures proper status in the community for the convert. We, however, are concerned with the sensitivity of converts at a later time. Two discussions provide some insight into this question. All converts receive a Hebrew name. Although nothing is said about this in the major codes, it has become a general custom. New male converts are generally named "the son of Abraham"; Abraham is considered the father of all proselytes (*Tanhuma Lekh Lekha* 32, ed. Buber). Although this custom is frequently followed (*Shulhan Arukh, Even Haezer* 129.20; Felder, *Nahalat Tzevi* 1.31, 124), it is not mandatory, nor is anything said about naming female proselytes, although we often name them "the daughter of Ruth," the most famous Biblical female proselyte. As such names are publicly used particularly in the *Torah* service, they are a public reminder of conversion.

We should also remember that individuals who are converted as infants may be given the opportunity to determine their own religious status at the age of maturity (*Bar Mitzvah* for boys and slightly easier for girls). They may reject Judaism without prejudice, if they wish (*Shulhan Arukh, Yoreh Deah* 268.7). This has made it necessary for the status of young convert to be remembered. Traditionally, there have been some matters of marriage law which specifically involve converts. They have been given broader latitude about whom they may marry, and this includes individuals of doubtful descent (*Kid.* 72b; *Shulhan Arukh, Even Haezer* 4.22). In this discussion, tradition has stated that this special status would continue until the tenth generation, or until the fact that "the family stemmed from a proselyte had been forgotten." A number of famous individuals have been specifically recalled as proselytes (Adiabne and Antipater in Josephus *Antiquities* XX 2; Onkelos in *Meg.* 3a; etc.).

Conversion to Judaism remains public knowledge. However, there is no intent to embarrass the convert. It would, therefore, be proper to have a public register of all life cycle events and conversions in the congregational library, yet it should be placed in such as way that it will not be used simply to satisfy idle curiosity.

*Walter Jacob, *Contemporary American Reform Responsa*, New York, 1987, #46.

UNPROVABLE CLAIMS TO CONVERSION

Solomon B. Freehof

QUESTION: A man aged forty-five has been married for several months. His wife is seeking an annulment of their marriage on the grounds that he misrepresented himself as a Jew at the time of the marriage. The man claims to be a Jew and has considered himself a Jew all his life. His mother was born a non-Jewess. His father, now eighty, states that his wife (the man's mother) was converted by a Reform rabbi before their marriage. He can find no record of it. To add to the difficulty, the mother, now deceased, was buried in a non-Jewish cemetery. The son (who is now being sued for annulment) was circumcised at a *Berit Milah*, was *Bar Mitzvah*, and married by a Conservative rabbi. He was reared as a Jew and considers himself a Jew. He is contesting the annulment on the grounds that if he does not, he will be indicating that he does not believe himself to be a Jew. Is the man to be considered a Jew or not, as far as Jewish law is concerned? (Rabbi Selig Salkowitz, Reform Temple of Fair Lawn, Fair Lawn, New Jersey)*

ANSWER: The problem is complicated. There are a number of crucial elements involved. The woman, who declares herself to be Orthodox, has evidently been instructed to contest the validity of the conversion of her husband's mother by a Reform rabbi. If that conversion is invalid, her husband is the son of a Gentile and has misrepresented himself as a Jew. Therefore, the first important question is the validity of a Reform conversion.

It might be too much to expect a strictly Orthodox rabbi to acknowledge the validity of any Reform ceremony which varies from the norm laid down in the *Shulhan Arukh*. A Reform conversion certainly does not conform to that norm. The fact that we may instruct the candidate for conversion much more thoroughly in Jewish beliefs and history than any Orthodox rabbi would instruct her would be immaterial in the face of the fact that we generally omit the *ceremonial* requirement of sending her to the ritual bath (*miqveh*). It is the ritual that matters to the Orthodox rabbi and not whatever intellectual and moral prescription we may give her. While, therefore, the absence of the ritual bath prevents the Orthodox rabbi from acknowledging the validity of our conversion, the courts have no right to question it and to assume that there is only *one* authentic form of Judaism and that is Orthodoxy. With regard to our ceremonial disagreement with Orthodoxy, there is nothing for decent people to do but endure it, and learn somehow to achieve mutual respect. So the question of the wife's refusal to acknowledge the authenticity of Reform conversion cannot be discussed with her. It can only be discussed in the courts, if necessary.

It is not only the Reform conversion which is here brushed aside; it is also the acceptance of the boy as a Jew by the Conservative rabbi which is here deemed irrelevant. The boy was circumcised as a Jew, was *Bar Mitzvah*, lived as a Jew. What objection is there, then, to considering him a Jew? It can only be that an Orthodox rabbi, rejecting the validity of the mother's conversion, considers this boy to be a Gentile, and therefore in addition to being circumcised, he should have been sent to the *miqveh*. It would be on this basis only that the boy's Jewishness could be denied. Again, it is the omission of a ceremonial which weighs more than the boy's Jewish education, *Bar Mitzvah*, and his whole life as a Jew.

However, there is another question which involves a complicated problem in Jewish law. This problem revolves around the fact that the man's father, now very old, can adduce no proofs that his wife was converted, as he claims she was. Such unprovable claims to conversion have evoked considerable discussion in the *Talmud* and in the Codes. The chief source of the laws involved is the *Talmud* in *b. Yevamot* 47a, and then the *Tur* and the *Shulhan Arukh* in *Yoreh Deah* 268:10 and 11. The various subdivisions of the problem are these: (a) a man claims to have been converted fore a certain Jewish court; (b) a man claims to have been converted privately, not before a court; (c) a man was assumed to be a Jew but now he himself has raised a question and says he has been a Gentile but has been converted; (d) a man was assumed to be a Gentile but claims that he has been converted.

These various situations arouse different reactions in the minds of the legal authorities. In general, their answer is that the man claiming to have been converted, let us say privately (without the technical requirements which the court would demand), has a right to cast doubt upon his own Jewishness by raising this question, but he has no right to cast doubt upon the Jewish status of his children. That is to say, before he may now marry another Jewess he would need to take a ritual bath (assuming that he is already circumcised), but, since at the time that he makes the statement he is not surely Jewish, he is not eligible to testify in a Jewish court against his children. The children are of unquestioned Jewish status.

There is some difference in the answers for each of the various categories mentioned above. But in general the tendency of the law is increasingly to accept a man's statement if he says he has been converted. Thus Asher ben Yehiel in the "*Pisqei Harosh*" 4:34, 35, sums up the law to his time when he says: if a man claims that he was converted before a certain court, he must bring proof (since a court's actions are susceptible of proof), but all the proof that is needed is merely for people to say, "We have heard that he was converted." Further, if a man says he was converted privately, he has to take the ritual bath before marrying a Jewess, but his sons are held to be Jewish. To *Tur, Yoreh Deah* 368, Joel Sirkes

(Bach) says: "At all events, it is our custom to believe the man's claims and even to marry him to a Jewess." Then Joel Sirkes proceeds to explain away partially the objections of Maimonides against believing the man. Joel Sirkes' statement is cited with approval by Sabbatai Cohen (*Shakh*, to *Shulhan Arukh, Yoreh Deah* 368:10 and 11). Sirkes to the *Tur* also quotes the well-known legal authority Moses, of Coucy, in his *S'Mag*, who says: "This occurs every day. Strangers come (and claim to be Jews). We do not bother to investigate. We drink wine with them and eat meat from their slaughtering." This general tendency of the law to accept the claim of a man that he is a Jew is reflected in a recent responsum by Isaac ben Aryeh Rudnik (*S'dei Yitzhaq*, London, 1961). The case with which he deals is that of a soldier who came to England from overseas, who claimed to be a Jew, married a Jewess; then his wife left him and lived with another man. Rabbi Rudnik decides that the marriage to the soldier who said he was a Jew is valid enough as Jewish marriage to require a Jewish divorce (*get*).

Of course, all this discussion involves the claimed conversion of a *man*. Our case here involves a woman whose conversion to Judaism is disputed. Nevertheless, the *Shulhan Arukh* understands that the above laws apply equally to man and woman. It cites the *Talmudic* law as follows (*Yoreh Deah* 268:10): "If a Gentile man or a Gentile woman come and say, 'I have been converted'...," and so forth. The spirit of the law is clear. It reveals a growing tendency to accept the claim of a person or a family to be Jewish. Furthermore, there is an overriding presumption in all such claims that families are assumed to be kosher (Jewish and legitimate) unless, of course, there is strong ground for doubt. This principle is stated in the *Talmud* (*Qiddushin* 76b).

Therefore, aside from Orthodox refusal to accept any conversion other than their own, a refusal which it is futile to debate, the overwhelming tendency of Jewish law in matters of unprovable claims for conversion is to accept the claim and to consider the person a Jew.

*Solomon B. Freehof, *Recent Reform Responsa*, Cincinnati, 1963, #17.

THE COURSE OF STUDY FOR *GERUT*

Walter Jacob

QUESTION: Several members of a congregation have questions about the conversion of a woman who has recently joined the congregation. She has moved to our city from another state and they claim that the study which led to her conversion was insufficient. Upon investigation it was discovered that the woman in question was converted to Judaism after only an afternoon of instruction. She followed the normal ritual of conversion with the appropriate witnesses. Since that time she has lived as a Jewess and since her arrival in this city she has attended the synagogue with some regularity and affiliated almost immediately. May her conversion be questioned? (Ernest Levi, Los Angeles, CA)*

ANSWER: For many decades the North American Reform movement has provided a fairly uniform course of study for conversion. This has been followed in most communities throughout the country. The length of time spent studying may vary from six to eight months as may the intensity of the instruction provided. The intent, however, has been to give the convert a reasonable background of the major aspects of Judaism and an understanding of basic concept, holidays, practices, liturgy and theology. There have, of course, been deviations from this norm usually due to very specific circumstances, as for example a perspective convert who has long been active in the Jewish community or one who has privately studied Judaism for years; under such circumstances the normal course would be redundant.

In all instances the primary consideration remains the intent of the individual to convert. If intent is present and sincere then it will usually be accompanied by a desire to learn far more than the introductory course. A major aspect of our courses is the exposure of the convert to many aspects of Judaism which may test his/her sincerity in ways which could not be anticipated. The course of study, therefore, is important both for what is learned and the additional level of sincerity which it elicits.

In this instance we must say that there really was no course of study at all and this perspective convert was hurriedly moved through the ritual. *Bedi-avad*, the conversion is valid. This is in keeping with the traditional sources which simply stated that a few major and a few minor commandments were taught to the perspective convert. He/she was asked whether they accepted the commandments, and that was followed by ritual of conversion (*M. Nedarim* 3.11; *B K* 5.4; *Shulhan Arukh, Orah Hayyim* 199.4). We can see that in previous times the instruction was much less formal although, of course, the perspective convert had to be warned and discouraged, but if he/she persisted the authorities accepted the individual.

In this instance the life pattern of the woman in question has indicated that she is serious about conversion. She has made Judaism very much part of her existence, she participates in the synagogue and has been actively involved in the Jewish community. We should encourage her to participate in adult education programs; she will probably do so anyhow. There is no reason to question her conversion. It is valid and must be accepted.

*Walter Jacob, *Questions and Reform Jewish Answers*, New York, 1992, #124.

THE PROSELYTE AND HER GENTILE PARENTS

Solomon B. Freehof

QUESTION: A young woman has come to be converted. She intends to marry a Jewish young man. Her parents favor her conversion. However, the couple, when married, intend to move to Israel. Her parents are firmly opposed to that plan. Is the attitude of the parents likely to create enough difficulties to the marriage that the rabbi would be justified in refusing to convert the young woman? (Rabbi Mark Staitman, Pittsburgh, Pennsylvania.)*

ANSWER: The situation as described does indeed involve potential bitterness and family division. Whether or not these probabilities should concern the rabbi depends first of all on the question as to whether the acceptance of the proselyte in Judaism is a mandatory duty (as, for example, it is in Christianity). The consensus of opinion seems to be that we are not mandated (as Christians are) to go and seek proselytes, but that is a worthy person comes to be converted, it is our duty to convert him (the discussion in *New Reform Responsa*, p. 73.). Therefore, in this case, since there may be difficulties involved, some of which may possibly lead the young wife to leave her husband, or to return to her former religious affiliation under the influence of her parents, the rabbi is justified in his hesitation and this is the basis for the question.

Perhaps the best way to clarify the situation is to assume for the sake of discussion that the young woman has already been converted and has been married to the Jewish young man. Now, he wants her to move to Israel with him. We pass over the question for the moment of the acceptability of a Reform conversion in Israel and assume that the form of this conversion will not be an impediment to their settlement there is that is their wish.

We were not told by the questioner what the young woman's own attitude is with regard to moving to Israel. We will assume that she is willing to do so. However, her parens are firmly opposed to the move. This sharp difference of opinion between them may, of course, intensify and embitter all involved and even endanger the marriage and the stability of the conversion. This may well be, but it need not necessarily be so. As long as the young bride can remain bound in her love to her parents, she may well keep communications open with them and perhaps ultimately establish some agreement. Therefore, the question now arises: How close, according to Jewish law, may a convert remain to her parents?

The bare statement of the law would seem to indicate that having been converted, she no longer has any relationship with the parents. The wording of the law is: A convert is a newborn child (*Yevamot* 22a). That is to say, like a newborn child, she has no past. What she was, what her relations were, no longer exist (incidentally, this must be the background of the expression in the Gospel: ("Unless you are like little children, you cannot enter the kingdom of heaven.") Therefore, since by this bald statement of the law she no longer has any kinship with her Gentile parents, she could now be permitted to marry any of her former close kin, or would no longer have duty which all children have to respect and honor her parents. Therefore, the law has been immediately modified for otherwise she could say, "Before I converted I could not marry those of close kinship to me but now do you permit it? Before I converted I was in duty bound to honor my parents, and now do you say I am no longer obligated to do so?" It is because of these potential protests on the part of the convert that the law was modified at once and as it stands now she must still consider herself akin to her parents and must continue to honor them in every way (*Shulhan Arukh, Yoreh Deah* 241:9).

Therefore, in spite of the present disagreement between her and her parents as to settling in Israel, she is still duty bound by Jewish law to respect their opinion and keep in close relationship with them. Because of this continued family relationship, it may well be that the disagreements can be fully and peaceably discussed and eventually settled to everyone's satisfaction.

Let us say now that she had been willing to go to Israel but that after discussing the move with her parents, she has changed her mind and is now opposed to the move. Does her refusal violate Jewish law? Is she in duty bound by the *halakhah* to accompany her husband to Israel? The original law stated (*Mishnah Qetubot*, last chapter) is that a husband may compel a wife to move to Israel with him; and if she refuses, he may divorce her without even giving her the *ketubah* amount. But this law has been almost completely modified. The *Tosfot* (*Qetubot* 110b) says that the law does not apply any more since roads are now dangerous (this was said in the 11th century). Joseph Caro (*Shulhan Arukh, Even Haezer* 74:4f) compromises and says that if the journey to Palestine is short and safe, as from Alexandria, he may compel her to join him, otherwise not. The *Be-er Hetev* sums up the law as follows: "Since whether he can compel her or not is a subject of disagreement among many authorities, he no longer can compel her to accompany him." Therefore, we may conclude that if after they are married, she changed her mind because of her parents' influence and refuses to go to Israel, she has committed no sin, and that from this point of view also, there is no objection to converting her. (See the full discussion in *Contemporary Reform Responsa* p. 69ff.)

To sum up: Since the bond and relationship with her parents will indeed continue, and since the point of issue, settling in Israel, no longer involves a religious mandate, it is possible that the matter of settling in Israel may be satisfactorily decided either way. There is therefore no strong objection to the conversion.

*Solomon B. Freehof, *Today's Reform Responsa*, Cincinnati, 1990.

MEMORIALIZING CHRISTIAN RELATIVES

Walter Jacob

QUESTION: A Christian woman, converted to Judaism and married to a Jew, arranged for her parents and other (Gentile) relatives to be memorialized in the *Qaddish* list of the congregation which is read annually. She died, and her Jewish-born husband has since remarried. Now he wants the names of the Gentile relatives of his late wife removed from the *Qaddish* list. He and his late wife had children, so these names are the names of the grandparents and other relatives of the man's children. (Rabbi P. Irving Bloom, Mobile, Alabama.)*

ANSWER: There are a number of questions involved in this inquiry. First, is it proper to have the names of Christians on the regular memorial list for annual *Qaddish*? Second, has the husband - now that he has married again - any justification for wanting to remove these names? In other words, may his second wife have grounds for objecting that her husband is still memorializing the relations of his first wife? Third, since a contribution was made to the congregation for putting these names on the annual *Qaddish* list, is it now possible to rescind and cancel such a contribution and so remove the names?

First, as to saying *Qaddish* for Gentiles, and also as to the congregation keeping on the *Qaddish* list a Gentile relative of a convert, this question was discussed fully in the Conference *Yearbook*, vol. LXVII, 1957. One might imagine that there is no religious bond between a daughter and her Gentile father, since a convert is a "new-born child." However, Maimonides in *Hilkhot Mamrim*, V. 11, says (based upon the *Talmud*), that a convert should honor his Gentile father. Rabbi Aaron Walkin, in a responsum written in 1933, states that honoring his father involves saying *Qaddish* for him. Since a son may say *Qaddish* for his Jewish-born *apostate* father (who had wilfully deserted Judaism), then certainly a proselyte may say *Qaddish* for a Gentile father who is naturally following the religion in which he was brought up. So, too, Abraham Zvi Klein, a rabbi in Hungary (*Beerot Avraham* II), speaks of receiving a gift from a Gentile woman who wants her name memorialized (i.e., not even a relative of a convert), and he concludes: "There is no prohibition against recording her name and her good deed in the *Hevra Qadisha*, and we should recite an '*El male rachamim*' for her on *Yizqor* days."

As for the second question, there is some sort of justification for an objection on the part of the man, or of his second wife, to his first wife (and possibly also her relatives) being memorialized now the man is married to this second woman. This question has come up quite often in the literature and has been dealt with in *Reform Responsa*, p. 162. For example, Eleazer Deutsch (1850-1916) in his *Duda-ei Hasadeh*, 14, was asked whether a remarried man may recite *Yizqor* for his first wife. He says no, but that if it was the custom of the synagogue - as it is in some communities - for the cantor to read a list of *all the names* memorialized, there was no objection to the remarried man being present. The general conclusion of all who discussed the question is that such memorial rites as might occur at home (the *Yahrzeit* light, etc.) should certainly not be observed any more. In the synagogue, however, if there is no one to say *Qaddish* for his first wife, the husband may do so. Of course, if there are children, it is better that they should say *Qaddish*. In the question asked, the names include not only the name of the first wife, but those of her relatives, so the second wife can have less objection to their names being read than if it were the first wife's name alone. Furthermore, there *are* grandchildren who want to honor their grandparents, which certainly should be permitted.

Now there is the third question: Since a contribution was made to the congregation (a number of years ago) to put these names on the regular *Qaddish* list, and since the congregation had accepted this specific contribution, can it now undo this memorial and cancel it and remove the names? A related question was asked of me by Rabbi William Braude of Providence. It was with regard to a memorial window. Someone wanted to pay money to have its dedication changed. This could not be permitted. Once the gift has been accepted by the congregation, no donor has any authority over it. The conclusion to the question asked about the memorial window applies here: "Once the gift has been received by the congregation, the donor has no more rights over it." Of course, the congregation, has more rights in the matter than the original donor, but even if the congregation itself wanted to change the memorial donation from one purpose to another, the law is full of many restrictions as to just which changes they can make. There is no need to go into this complicated question.

From all the above, we come to the following conclusions: First, there is nothing wrong with a Gentile being permanently memorialized in the *Qaddish* list. Secondly, the husband - while justly sensitive to memorializing his first wife in the presence of his second wife - has no right to deprive his children of the privilege of memorializing their mother, grandparents, and other close relatives. Finally, once a gift has been received by the congregation, it is virtually impossible for an individual to have it changed, and there are considerable restrictions as to the right of the congregation itself.

*Walter Jacob, *American Reform Responsa*, New York, 1983, #125.

AN APOSTATE PROSELYTE

Walter Jacob

QUESTION: What is the status of a proselyte who has decided to return to his/her original religion? What is the status of the children?*

ANSWER: Any convert to Judaism has acquired an entirely new status. Indeed, the *Talmud* has compared a proselyte to a new-born child (*Yev.* 22a). He or she has not only adopted the faith of Israel, but has also become a part of the people of Israel. For this reason, it has been customary to name proselytes "The son or daughter of our Father Abraham (*Bet Yosef* on *Tur, Even Haezer* 129; *Shulhan Arukh, Even Haezer* 129.20; Felder, *Nahalat Tzevi* 1.31, 124) or Sarah, our Mother" (*Gates of Mitzvah*, p. 24). It is, therefore, the almost unanimous opinion that converts who revert to their original religions remain Jewish and are to be considered Jewish for all purpose (*Bekorot* 30b). Their status was the same as that of Jewish apostates. This problem has been dealt with again and again with the same conclusion (*Yev.* 47b; Asher Ben Yehiel, *ibid., Tur, Yoreh Deah* 268; *Shulhan Arukh, Yoreh Deah* 268.12, as well as the commentaries on these passages; Freehof, *Reform Responsa*, pp. 192ff). The *Shulhan Arukh* and most of its commentaries agree that the child of an apostate female proselyte, or of a male married to a Jewish woman, would be considered Jewish and would need no formal conversion to Judaism. An adult proselyte who has become a Jew voluntarily cannot annul this process in any was (*Shulhan Arukh, Yoreh Deah* 268.2, 12). Isserles indicated that the Rabbinic ordinances, however, demanded of an apostate returning to Judaism or the child of an apostate woman (who had been born or converted to Judaism), repentance before a court of three, as well as immersion in a *miqveh* (Radbaz, *Responsa III*, 415; Isserles to *Yoreh Deah* 268.12; Hoffman, *Melamed Lehoil II*, 84) for full acceptance into the Jewish community. Abraham Gumbiner (*Magen Avraham* to *Shulhan Arukh, Orah Hayyim* 326.8) reminded us that ritual immersion was not legally necessary, but was a fence around the law.

All this clearly indicates that Judaism does not recognize a permanent change in status away from the Jewish people. A convert reverting to another religion would be considered an apostate.

We cannot, of course, deny individuals the right to adopt a religion of their choice. They have the freedom to adopt Judaism and the freedom to leave it. For all practical purposes, they will then be outside the Jewish community (in contrast to *Bek.* 30b), but we would always be willing to accept their return to us. Their children too, will have full rights as Jews, should they wish to exercise them.

*Walter Jacob, *American Reform Responsa*, New York, 1983, #71.

CONTRIBUTORS

David Ellenson - I.A. and Anna Grancell Professor of Jewish Religious Thought at the Hebrew Union College - Jewish Institute of Religion in Los Angeles as well as visiting Professor of History at the University of California, Los Angeles. He has published *Tradition in Transition: Orthodoxy, Halakhah, and Boundaries of Modern Jewish Identity*, and *Rabbi Esriel Hildesheimer and the Creation of Modern Jewish Orthodoxy*. *Between Tradition and Culture* is scheduled for publication in 1994.

Solomon B. Freehof - (1893-1990), Rabbi of the Rodef Shalom Congregation, President of the Central Conference of American Rabbis and the World Union for Progressive Judaism, Chair of the Responsa Committee of the Central Conference of American Rabbis. Author of eight volumes of responsa including *Today's Reform Responsa* (1990), as well as *Reform Jewish Practice* (1947, 1952), *The Responsa Literature* (1955), *A Treasury of Responsa* (1963).

Walter Jacob - Rabbi of the Rodef Shalom Congregation, Pittsburgh, Immediate past President of the Central Conference of American Rabbis, President of the Freehof Institute of Progressive *Halakhah*. Author and editor of fourteen books including *American Reform Responsa* (1983), *Contemporary American Reform Responsa* (1987), *Liberal Judaism and Halakhah* (1988), *Questions and Reform Jewish Answers - New Reform Responsa* (1991).

Richard Rosenthal - Rabbi, Temple Beth El, Tacoma, Washington and Adjunct Professor at the University of Puget Sound. He has written essays on Jewish law.

Mark Washofsky - Associate Professor of Rabbinics - Hebrew Union College - Jewish Institute of Religion in Cincinnati. His publications include studies on the development of *halakhic* thought in medieval and modern times. He currently serves as Vice Chair of the Responsa Committee of the Central Conference of American Rabbis.

Moshe Zemer - Director of the Freehof Institute of Progressive *Halakhah*; a founder of the Movement for Progressive Judaism in Israel; *Av Bet Din* of the Israel Council of Progressive Rabbis; founding rabbi of Kedem Synagogue in Tel Aviv; author of forthcoming the book, *The Sane Halakhah* (Hebrew).

Bernard M. Zlotowitz - Rabbi and Senior Scholar for the Union of American Hebrew Congregations; doctorate in Septuagint from the Hebrew Union College - Jewish Institute of Religion. He writes the column, "Q & A" for *Reform Judaism*. Author many books as well as scholarly and popular articles.

www.ingramcontent.com/pod-product-compliance
Lightning Source LLC
Chambersburg PA
CBHW071959290426
44109CB00018B/2070